EDUMAGIC

A guide for pre-service teachers

Samantha Fecich

EduMagic
Samantha Fecich

Published by EduMatch®
PO Box 150324, Alexandria, VA 22315
www.edumatch.org

These books are available at special discounts when
purchased in quantity for use as premiums, promotions
fundraising, and educational use. For inquiries and
details, contact the publisher: sarah@edumatch.org.

ISBN: 978-1-970133-21-9

Shout Outs

Acknowledgments sound so formal to me. So, I would like to call this section shout outs! First and foremost, my family. Thank you to my husband Josh Fecich for your love and support. You are the love of my life and the man of my dreams. To Summer Fecich, my daughter, you are the little love of my life, and you are my summer sunshine. I love you. To my parents, Joe and Kathy Horochak, you've taught me so much about myself. The most important thing you taught me is how to dust myself off and keep trying. Thank you for believing in me. To my sister, Allie Ondash, thank you for your encouragement and keeping me grounded in all that I do.

Next, the amazing pre-service teachers, practicing educators, and colleagues who contributed to this book. Without your insights, wisdom, advice, and inspiration, this book would not be a reality. Thank you for adding your perspective – I greatly value it.

Finally, EduMatch, thank you for believing in my message and getting it out there. I hope that through this book, other pre-service teachers find their own edumagic and implement it into their own classrooms.

Table of Contents

Introduction: Once Upon a Time...

"You're a wizard, Harry."

– Harry Potter and the Philosopher's Stone

As you read this book, I want you to imagine that you and I are sitting in your favorite coffee shop. We just ordered our coffees (I prefer a pumpkin spice latte), and we are sitting down having a conversation about what it means to be a teacher while in college! So, take a sip, sit back, and let's chat.

The first day of class is always abuzz with excitement, anticipation, and nervousness for the semester and year to come. Students bustle around the hallways greeting one another with waves, high fives, and hugs. Others just keep their heads down, as if their coffee hasn't kicked in yet. There are still other students that look lost like a deer in the headlights. I spot those "lost deer" types since I teach at 8:00 am on Monday mornings and am usually the first class for a first-semester freshman. To be honest, the freshmen are easy to spot. They usually have their dorm keys on lanyards around their necks and are wearing a Grove City College t-shirt.

For me, the first day is not the usual first day of classes. While other professors are going over the syllabus, bullet point by bullet point, I have a class dedicated to mingling and getting to know each other. On the first day in a Dr. Fecich class, we greet, play games and just spend time in fellowship. While some professors are inside their classroom, I am outside of the classroom greeting students, waving, and welcoming them in whatever way I can to the new learning experiences that will take place in my course. I like to "think outside the bun" (my dad's favorite saying from old Taco Bell commercial). For instance, I shake their hands or give them a high five or a fist bump and welcome them to class. When they walk into the classroom, there is usually some sort of Taylor Swift song playing, and the stage has been set to mingle. Once all students have entered the classroom, I greet them again and make certain everyone is in the right room.

I am a firm believer in the old saying by Teddy Roosevelt, "people don't care how much you know until they know how much you care," which is so true for our students. We need to start day one with building those relationships, and with a culture of respect and rapport in our classrooms, no matter what subject area or grade level we teach! I have students introduce themselves to one another, answering typical questions (you know like that first date in college) such as name, major, year, hometown, etc. I add in questions like favorite songs, hidden talents, or birthdays just to jazz it up. In the past, I have had students draw a sketchnote of their introduction, and that is always a lot of fun to see. Sketchnotes are drawings showing ideas and concepts. In my case, I have students draw out their introductions and show us a bit about themselves instead of standing up and telling us. It is a great way to have them to start thinking creatively.

Once everyone introduces him/herself, I usually

stop the class and say something like, "Five bonus points to the entire class if someone can stand up and name everyone in the class." The expressions on their faces change so quickly as they look around at their peers' confused faces and try to remember names. Since I teach pre-service teachers, I can use this as an opportunity to show them that knowing (your) students is so important, and calling them by their name is critical in starting that relationship.

It is so sad to sit in a class and not know the names of the people around you. I challenge you to get to know one another because the relationships in life will carry you far. You all have the same end goal in mind – to become educators of excellence.

> Challenge:
> Get to know your people (and learn with them).

Don't stop at getting to know your peers. Also, reach out to your professors. I truly enjoy getting to know my students outside of class. I love grabbing a cup of coffee or lunch with someone in my class and just learning about their story and what brought them to the field of education.

You can do the same. Find a professor that you enjoy and just ask, "Hey, can we get a cup of coffee sometime? I would love to get to know ya." Or perhaps if you think that is too forward, use the formal form of "you" and send an email. Please don't hesitate to get to know your professors – trust me we are people too!

Personally, I try to make time for people; open my

3

door to let others in and share what is on their hearts – it is never time wasted. The seeds that you plant now in someone's life will grow farther than you may ever know. You must invest in people and in relationships. When you invest in others, the rewards you get back are priceless.

Whether you are just starting out or ready to take the plunge, I am excited to share some ideas that can help you put some *edumagic* into your college career. All the advice in this book is things that I wish I could tell my younger self when I was studying to be an educator. I hope that this book inspires, encourages, and pushes you to become an educator like no other! An educator that only *you* can be.

Your guide to harnessing your EduMagic

Just something to note – in this book I refer to pre-service teachers as future teachers or teachers in training. This term refers to students of any age learning about what it takes to become an educator of excellence. Although this book is geared towards pre-service teachers, the advice, tips, techniques, and stories can reignite any educator's passion for teaching and learning.

This book is separated into eight parts – each section includes advice from pre-service educators just like you, challenges, and follow up activities and questions. Please tweet out accomplishments from your journey using the hashtag #edumagic. I look forward to seeing how you create some *edumagic* in your college career!

E: Educate and engage

This section is all about how you can approach courses in college and make the most of your college career.

D: Digital presence

It is your digital presence, you should own it NOW! Tips, tricks, and strategies are shared in this chapter how you can harness the power of your digital presence for good!

U: Unite your PLN

Every quest is better with a friend to two. Dive into this chapter and learn how to gather your questing buddies. They can help you along the way, provide you with encouragement, and challenge you to the best educator you can be!

M: Megapixels

This is not a unit of resolution for a picture, but instead a term my dad uses to refer to sprinkles. In this chapter, you will learn about how to take those ordinary lessons and sprinkle some magical pixie dust on them.

A: Always be...

This chapter is a montage of sayings on just how to be a good teacher while in college. It includes stories about how to always be mindful, gracious, kind, and an advocate.

G: Get out!

Get out is one of my favorite chapters. It is divided into three parts: Get out of the classroom, get out of your regularly scheduled program, and get out of your comfort zone.

J: Inconceivable

Technology makes the impossible, possible. This chapter includes how technology can be integrated to engage students in learning experiences like no other!

C: Co-ops gone virtual

This chapter is all about the virtual co-op program and its origin. It details stories from pre-service teachers and their co-operating in-service teachers. The virtual co-op program has many wins – you will have to read about it to learn more.

Your journey has been laid out before you, and as you embark upon your path know this: you are a professional educator. It is a little secret you need to discover now! As soon as you leap over that hurdle and embrace the mindset that you are a professional – the sooner you can begin to knock down walls. Just as Harry Potter discovers that he is a wizard, you have the magic within you already to be an educator of excellence. You may have just stepped into your first undergraduate course to learn how to be a teacher, but you, my friend, are a professional educator.

E – Educate and Engage

During our first edcamp at Grove City College, we did a large group activity where attendees participated in a "Why I Teach" activity. Each participant wrote their response to the title prompt on a cartoon thought bubble. Participants then shared their reasons through social media using the conference hashtag. PreK-4 pre-service teacher Emily Wilson tweeted why she wanted to be an educator, "Because teaching is the profession that creates all other professions." Think about that! Seriously. You are going to impact future authors, scientists, cartoonist, engineers, nurses, baristas, filmmakers, ice cream taste testers, lawyers, stunt people, sales representatives, doctors, dog walkers, and teachers. You! You are going to be teaching our next generation of innovators! That is an incredible calling!

My question to you is, "Why do you teach?" Whoa, that is a loaded question. Why do you want to be an educator? Stop reading at this point and seriously answer that question. Go ahead...you may want to document your answer in one of the margins. Here, I'll make some space for you. *because it creates all other professions*

When I ask my students about this seemingly simple question, I usually get one of two answers. I either get "I love kids," or "I've wanted to be a teacher for as

7

long as I can remember." Then they go on to share how they would play school with their stuffed animals. Those aren't wrong answers – I mean you wouldn't be a teacher if you didn't at least like kids, but I'm looking for something deeper.

Think about your answer – was it similar? Is this going to be your answer to a future employer? What makes you stand out from the other candidates who also love children? What have you done or what will you do to impact the lives of children? Most teachers love kids, but what makes you different? Dig deep. Feeling brave? Tweet out your message and let the world know why you are an educator. Don't forget to add #edumagic and tag me (@Sfecich) in your tweet!

Someone once told me, "Samantha, some people are born to teach, and you are not one of them." These words were spoken to me during my second student teaching placement as an undergraduate student teacher by my college supervisor. I was truly enjoying my student teaching in an inner-city school. My first placement was with students who were pulled out for learning support in reading. In that seventh- and eighth-grade class, we created a crime scene where students had to use context clues to find out who took the principal's badge.

In my second student teaching placement, I was in a fifth-grade class where we were reading *The Wizard of Oz* (Baum, 1900), one of my favorite books. In this class, I planned cross-curricular activities and brought Oz to life, literally! I created a green throne room that students entered by transforming the entrance of the classroom into a castle. Students got to walk through Emerald City and visit different stations. During math class, students used their money skills to count out the correct amounts and gave change to buy green candy in Emerald City. Yes, they actually bought green candy. It was an amazing and challenging learning experience.

So, you may be thinking to yourself, "Hmmm... Ok, Sam, those examples you gave were awesome but why would someone say that?" Honestly, you guys, I don't know. I told you that story so you would understand that "...words have power, but our actions shape our lives." (Hollis, 2018). Yes, it would have been easy to have given up and thrown in the towel, to give up on the dream that I had to teach kids. But I didn't. I got knocked down and got back up again (cue the song "Tubthumping" [Chumbawumba, 1997] here). Trust me, friends, you too will be knocked down, but it is up to you to get up, brush it off, and try again. Ok, let's get back to it.

So, why do I teach? When I was beginning college, I thought teaching was about:

- Working 8:00 AM – 3:00 PM.
- Having summers off.
- No homework – that is for the students.
- Get a week off for Christmas and Easter.
- Two-hour delays and snow days.
- Write one lesson for each class for the year, and I'm done! Then keep reusing that lesson over and over again.

Yes! Seriously, I thought this. Oh, younger

Sammie, you were so naive. Luckily, I was shown the light and the error of my ways. I was wrong! I know now that teaching is a 24/7 job – whether we are grading papers, providing feedback to our students, writing a positive note home, or just thinking about that one child in our class who may be going through some rough stuff.

Having summers off – I wish! We spend our summers revising lesson plans and getting our classes ready for the next school year. Our lesson plans need to be altered, adapted, changed, and modified to fit the needs of our students. Although we may get time off for Christmas and Easter, we still have parties to plan and gifts to give. As for the two-hour delays…we all know that we still need to try to be here at the appropriate time, two-hour delay or not. And as for snow days…we have to make those up in the summer! I learned all of these lessons during my first year of teaching at Clairview School.

At Clairview, a school for students with special needs in Pennsylvania, I taught students with multiple disabilities. I wanted to be an educator who helps students find their voices through augmentative and alternative communication (AAC) devices. An AAC device helps students who can't physically speak communicate by using specialized equipment. I guess you can say, I taught for the smiles.

What do I mean by that? Well, in my class we made a Thanksgiving feast for the parents one year. We had students using environmental controls (devices that hook up to a special switch to activate a device that you plug into a wall – in this example, a blender) to blend mashed potatoes. Students poured bags of frozen veggies into a baking dish, we made pudding for dessert, and of course, we had turkey. Parents and administrators joined us around the table in our classroom, and we enjoyed a feast. It was such a powerful way to show everyone that these kids can do amazing things. This would not have been possible without an amazing team of personal care aides, classroom assistants, and nurses. We pulled together and helped to make things happen with our kids.

One of my favorite memories was using the interactive whiteboard (SMART board). My class was the first class to use the SMART board. In fact, I pulled it out of the closet one day, and it stayed in my classroom for the rest of the year. We used it to practice calendar skills, attendance, fine and gross motor skills, literacy, numeracy, and other topics. I figured if my students can use it, then other students in the school could too! That is what brought me into my second placement at Clairview as the Instructional Technology Coach.

I started teaching instructional technology by pushing into the classrooms at Clairview. Students used laptops, iPods (they were cool at the time), Flip video cameras, the Wii gaming system, and interactive whiteboards. Students even took over the morning news announcements on the school TV. Students learned 21st-century learning skills like communication, collaboration, and creativity through using technology effectively and efficiently. In addition to teaching students, I also provided professional development to the faculty and staff on a variety of educational technology tools. This is where my thoughts about why I teach changed. I still taught for the smiles and the use of educational technology to support learning, but I wanted to grow more and to share my knowledge with other educators. I enjoyed teaching other teachers so much that I decided to pursue my PhD in learning design and technology at Penn State University.

Now I am teaching future educators at Grove City College. My reason for becoming a professor has been influenced by my amazing colleagues, like my mentor, Connie Nichols. She teaches to impact classrooms that she will never see through the work of our pre-service educators. I want to do the same, raising up the next generation of teachers to become educators of excellence with some *edumagic* sparkle.

I teach to be like my mentors, such as Jackie Hammill, my middle school chorus teacher. She showed patience with all her students, no matter their singing ability. When I was trying out for chorus, I walked in ready to sing "Happy Birthday." I sang as loud and as high as I could. I wanted to be a soprano because I thought being an alto meant that you were "out of" the chorus. Mrs. Hammill helped me find the error of my ways. She used humor and would use relative topics to get our attention in her music class. She valued student voice and choice in the numbers that we sang.

Cindy Shaffer, my supervisor at Clairview School, showed me the importance of how passion can drive advocacy. She advocated for educational technology, and we worked together to apply and receive grants for the school. Together we integrated technology tools into the lives of students and teachers.

Funding is hard. When you are a teacher, you are often spending your own money to fund your classroom. Take it from me, try to write a grant or two to help with big-ticket items.

I remember one summer day, I was cruisin' around Twitter and someone from my PLN posted a contest for Lenovo computers, where all you had to do was write a blurb about how you can use the computers in your classroom. So, I thought, "What the heck?"

I spent an hour or so writing a short explanation of what I did as a special education teacher and how I would use the computers in my classroom (they were touchscreens – and mind you in the early 2000s those were cutting edge!). A few months passed, and I forgot all about it until one day I received an email stating that I won six Lenovo computers!

Holla!

I was pumped. When I received the news, I decided to put a computer in each of the multiple disabilities and autistic support classrooms in my school. It was awesome to be able to help give access to the internet through the touch screen computers because some of the students were unable to use a mouse. Being able to touch the screen made a world of difference. Now students could access educational material independently! The adrenaline rush of knowing my time spent had such a huge impact on student learning has become a big part of my "why."

It is so important to keep your "why" in mind when you are an education major. It is like a hot cup of coffee during an 8:00 A.M. exam in winter – it will keep you fueled. Think back to your why. Why are you a teacher? Why are you impacting students? Schools? Districts? Countries? The world? You may be thinking to yourself, "The world? Yeah right, come on Sam. The world? I am just a teacher." You are NEVER just a teacher. You have the power to influence the lives of your students for better or worse, for good or bad. That my friend, is the secret. You can impact the world. Don't let anyone say that you can't!

Now I know some of you may be thinking, "Ok I can keep focused on my 'why' when it comes to education-related courses, that is easy." Not so fast. Yes, it is easier to focus on your "why" when you are in classes that are teaching you strategies, techniques, pedagogies, tools, etc. to add to your teacher toolbelt. But sometimes the best pre-service teacher can take a day off of being on their "A" game. Take it from me, sometimes it isn't that easy to stay focused in your education courses. I remember in college I would cram for tests the night before, I always regretted that. If I could go back, I would tell my younger self: *don't cram*! It is going to help you in the short term but not the long term. Instead, go over your notes each night after classes.

The only reason I crammed was to get the A in the class, but I would love to tell my younger self and you that it's not about the A! Please don't strive for the A or be all about the points, it's about the learning – not the A. Please, learn this lesson now. Let me say it again, but in different words so it sinks in a little deeper. Courses are not about getting the A, it's NOT about getting all the points or getting 100% in a class. Yes, a good GPA is important, but what is more important is what you learned as a result of a class. What do you have to show for your learning?

You might be thinking, "Ok. I get it, it's about the learning. I can get motivated to learn in education courses because I will need that information when I graduate. But what about general education classes that everyone must take? When am I ever going to need to know how to weave a basket underwater? I am never going to need this!" Or maybe an assignment is just busy work, and you are never going to use it in your own classroom. Honestly, it is so easy to fall into that mindset. But you must keep your eye on the prize to educate and engage yourself in the class as a teacher! Ask yourself, "how could I teach this content to my future students?" Or, "will my future students need to know this?" Don't be so quick to judge the importance of an assignment based upon your past experiences. I challenge you to go beyond yourself and figure out the professor's "why" regarding an assignment. Why does the professor think it is important for you to know? Why must you be able to understand these skills or steps?

Hannah Mercer, a pre-service teacher studying elementary education, shares that when given what can seem like busy work at first glance, she initially sees how this idea or concept could apply to her classroom, whether that be in content or practice. If she is unable to see a direct connection to her future classroom, she then tries to take a different perspective to envision how she could use it to help motivate or inspire her future students. For example, if you are struggling with an assignment, use it to grow and practice. Then, you will be able to share the experience with your students about how you overcame and persisted through a difficult problem.

Another way to educate and engage like a teacher is to think about the skills that go into creating the product or process, broadening your view from just content-driven outcomes to the processes along the way. This means focusing on how to solve a problem, or on the skills that go into research and writing. Let's take biology, for example. You may not be teaching those topics to elementary students, but you can teach them the skills of critical thinking, reflecting, revising, experimenting, trying things out, failing forward, etc. It is important to show our students that processes and skills are sometimes just as important as the answer or the product.

Catherine Root, a sophomore PreK-4 major shares that, "although you may never touch calculus again, the problem-solving skills that you acquire will assist in helping you succeed later in life." Abbey Mae Method, a recent graduate in secondary biology, adds, "I find it helpful to see the value in the process behind the assignment. When there is an assignment that reinforces content that I may never use again, I remind myself that the habits and principles taught through the process–task analysis, detail orientation, critical thinking, and even just pure diligence–will make me a better professional and life-long learner. Also, to learn to have grace, patience, and a good attitude amidst the frustration allows one to have a better platform to work from the inside to change the system and be an effective professional."

This is so true! You can also use these ideas in

your future classroom to show your students persistence, perseverance, effort, and resiliency. By doing this, you are modeling a growth mindset for your students. Jessie Pyle, a middle-level education major, shared that she believes that demonstrating this type of mindset to students is essential in today's society, as it goes beyond the classroom and helps them see the good things in a variety of situations.

Finally, if you feel like you are in a class with Ben Stein, learning about economics from *Ferris Bueller's Day Off* (Hughes, 1986), then I suggest thinking about the pedagogy being displayed. Are there some strategies that you could use in your future classroom? Meaning are there existing strategies that this teacher is employing that could be effective?

During every class, I aim to model student engagement and foster a positive classroom environment built on respect and rapport. When I teach, I showcase different types of strategies and pedagogies for my students, so they get to experience them and can use them in their own classes if they wish. Some examples:

- Edcamp-style: students choose a subtopic to discuss in smaller groups, and we do group rotations every few minutes
- Virtual classes with online discussion boards
- Small group presentations
- Large group discussions
- Think/pair/tweet – students individually think and reflect on a prompt, chat with a

17

neighbor about it, and co-create a tweet tagging them both in it with the class hashtag

- App smackdowns – students have one minute to showcase a favorite tech tool
- Scavenger hunts using technology tools like QR codes or <u>GooseChase</u>
- Speed-dating class related to syllabus topics – students are discussing content related to the course in a speed dating style. This is a great way to engage in conversation and introduce the course.
- Sketchnotes and gallery walk – students draw out a sketchnote of an ISTE Standard for Educators (2017) and an ISTE Standard for Students (2016), and we hang them up around the room. Then we go around the room with sticky notes and comment on the work.
- Stations
- Guest speakers – hearing a different voice from a professional in the field brings in a fresh perspective or new way of thinking. It is a great way to connect pedagogy, practice, and theory. I have had guest speakers join us in person and via Skype. This is a great practice for students to know and see, "Hey I can bring in experts into my class too via Skype." Also, they hear how a strategy that we are learning in our class is applied in a real class with

actual students.

By experiencing a variety of methods and strategies, students can find some that resonate with them to replicate in their own classes. Emily Bach, a recent graduate in Pre-K-4 elementary education with a specialization in Spanish, shares her experience when she was in a class where time felt like it was ticking backward.

> I tried to find points that I would either emulate in the teacher's style or elements that I would discard in my own teaching. There is value in learning almost anything. Stretching our brains enables us to see the world around us better and develop soft skills like grit and resilience, self-control, and metacognition.

Challenge:
Make a list of strategies to use in your own classroom.

You may want to keep a list of strategies that you are observing for future reference. Seriously, write it down! While you may have an excellent memory, keeping a written list will ensure the things you wanted to try will be readily accessible when you are ready for them. For example, in graduate school, I had a document labeled "Future College Class," where I kept a list of strategies or techniques that my professors used during class that I would want to try in my college class one day!

Another suggestion is to create a shared document with other students, so you can all take collaborative notes. This is a great strategy to get other perspectives about ideas or concepts. In fact, I did this in graduate school where we all took shared notes and added in comments or examples of the concepts in the margins. This provided us with a rich document of notes, ideas, examples, and strategies. It also gave us a great study guide when it came to writing a paper or taking a test.

I work hard to provide pre-service teachers with meaningful work and assignments. I want my class, the work that they do to be a learning experience that will benefit them. One of my favorite assignments was just this past semester, where a class of junior pre-service special education teachers worked with the vocational-technical (*vo-tech*) education department at a local school for at-risk male youth. Before developing the assignment, I was in a meeting with the Education Department Chair at Grove City College, Connie Nichols, and Deb Armstrong, teacher and professional development leader for the residential school. We were discussing ways technology could be used to enhance teaching and engage students. As a team, we brainstormed ideas to try with the vo-tech courses.

From there, our idea was born. I happened to be teaching a class of junior special education majors the following semester – this would be a great project for them! They had the experience and knowledge of how to adapt materials for students with special needs and how to use technology effectively. It was perfect.

Deb Armstrong came to speak with my class about the school, giving them insights about some needs that we could help with. Students were then divided into teams and paired with a vo-tech teacher (masonry, carpentry, welding, cooking, etc.). During the next class, we took a tour of the vo-tech facility and met with the faculty. My students (the pre-service teachers) took pictures and video of equipment used in the shop. They used those photos and videos in their adapted presentations. They then created interactive and engaging PowerPoint presentations that walked the high school students through paperwork, course materials, questions, and content related to the class using voice over technology, related images, graphics, and video clips.

The presentations read aloud words on the screen and brought to life images from the textbook. The vo-tech teachers utilized the PowerPoints with their students during class time as a way for students to read through the content of the book.

This assignment was very meaningful and impactful for the pre-service teachers as they had a direct hand in helping the vo-tech teachers with a problem in their classroom. I could have given them a case study and said, "create a PowerPoint on a reading area for this student." However, collaborating through real-world application of content and pedagogy in the field provided the pre-service teachers with a much richer, more meaningful, and lasting experience. By impacting actual classrooms and students, the work was high quality because it was being shared not just with me, but with teachers and students. It was being used in actual classrooms. This is an assignment that I will continue to do with my students through the years to come. It not only enriched my practice, but it gave my students an authentic learning activity. It also strengthened a relationship between the school and the college.

Sometimes we just must learn for the sake of learning, and not all assignments can have this much of a direct impact on students and teaching. Anna Emmons, a freshman secondary history education major shares that it is a fact of life we are not going to like or find value in EVERY assignment, and that is OK. She states, "as teachers, we should be striving to make sure that our classes are engaging and that our assignments are purposeful. Not all of our students are going to love our classes (and they definitely won't all love the things we assign)."

Naomi Shrom-Kuc, a PreK-4 and special education major, adds this encouraging word:

> Classes that do not seem to
> directly apply to my future work
> as a teacher give me an inside
> view into the life of my students.
> It increases my knowledge and
> teaches me the value of learning
> for its own sake.

Tasks like these teach me
diligence, time management, and
self-discipline. I often do not
recognize how much I am
learning through a task or a class
until I have time later to reflect on
it, or until I realize that I'm using
skills that I thought I would not
need.

This is so important to remember as an educator. My dad always said, "you don't know what you don't know." It is a simple statement, but it is so true. You don't know what you don't you know – how can you? That is why you must keep your mind open to new learning possibilities.

Challenge:
Don't be afraid to amp up your assignment to best benefit your learning. Go beyond the minimum requirements.

Instead of approaching an assignment as busy work, find yourself a virtual cooperating (co-op) teacher and create an authentic artifact for him or her to use in their classrooms (read more about a virtual co-op in Chapter 8: "Co-op Gone Virtual"). When you get an assignment to write a lesson plan about a topic of your choice, reach out to your PLN and contact a teacher and ask if you can write a lesson plan for a topic that s/he is covering in the class next. This will give you an authentic experience in writing a lesson plan on a topic that will be covered.

For example, if you are studying to be an elementary teacher and you are in a class where you need to write a science lesson for third graders, reach out to your PLN, find a third-grade science teacher, and develop a lesson plan based on a topic that s/he is covering next week. This will save you from having that mindset of busy work, and it gives you an authentic audience to work with. Another bonus is that you don't have to search your brain for what topics third graders are covering. Instead of having a lesson that is "meh," limited by your own experiences and your view of what is "typical" in a classroom, you now you have a lesson that you can showcase, and it will be used with real students.

Don't rely on your own experience as the only truth or way to do things. Don't just teach your students the way that you were taught – you are teaching a new generation of students. Think about that. Open your mind to new techniques, strategies, pedagogies, and tools. You never know what is going to work.

Want to bump it up a notch? Ask the teacher for feedback on how the lesson went, what went well, what can be improved upon, etc. Now let's add some sprinkles (or megapixels as my dad puts it) ...why not ask the teacher if you can visit the classroom or Skype in live to see how the lesson went, or even co-teach it virtually? Boom! Now you are a winner, and sprinkles are for winners. That would be awesome on so many levels: you get to teach students a lesson you created in an authentic atmosphere, you get immediate feedback, you get to teach in an online virtual atmosphere (if it isn't local), and *you get in front of kids* (I know I said the last one twice).

Think about it...you had the assignment of writing a lesson plan on a topic of your choice that you may or may not use again. This assignment was just for the professor to grade, and no one else will see this assignment. You would have gotten a grade on it, and that is it.

Is that truly meaningful for you? OK, you got an A, but now what? You don't know how it would work in a real classroom. But after accepting the challenge, you transformed it into a piece you can really showcase, something that is purposeful and authentic. That is adding some *edumagic* to your assignment.

So, Now What?

- 🖊 Think like a teacher in your classes, whether that be related to content, process, technique, strategy, or pedagogy. How will this content help your students? How would you teach this topic?
- 🖊 Keep a list (digitally or on paper) of strategies that you like, or techniques you observe that you would want to use in your own classroom.
- 🖊 Ditch the busy work mindset and make the assignment authentic for you! Go above and beyond, and don't look back.
- 🖊 When you have your own class, think about the purpose and meaning behind the work you are giving your students.

Starr Sackstein (2016) writes about the importance of rethinking homework and suggests several questions that educators should ask themselves before giving homework, some of them being: "How is the homework tied to the learning? Is it necessary? How does it support student learning?" Reflect if the assignment will genuinely help students understand the work or the skill. Consider if the assignment enhances learning.

D – Digital Presence

> *"It is important to remember that we all have magic*
> *inside us!"* — *J.K. Rowling*

One of my favorite assignments that I give my students is *"Google is the New Resume."* The assignment is simple (or is it?). Students search for their names on Google and reflect on what comes up in the search results. Students must type in their first and last name and share their results on a virtual bulletin board.

- How many hits do you have under each category (web, photos, videos, etc.)? How many of those hits are accurate?
- What can be improved upon?
- How do you feel about this experience ("It was lit," "meh," or "bummed out")?
- How do you rate your online presence?

When this assignment is due, students are usually whispering about what they found out about themselves online. To start the class, I have students share their results with a neighbor. I give them the following scenario: you are applying for your dream job, and you are Googled by the Assistant Superintendent. He finds these exact results. What would he think of you as a professional?

I ask you that same questions, think about it. What did Google come up with? How does it reflect on you as an educator? I encourage you to take some time to do the same thing. What comes up when you Google yourself? Go ahead document your results here.

Results for this assignment are mixed. Sometimes I have one or two students who find something that they would not want a future employer to see (like a photo or two). Yes, they are embarrassed by admitting this fact, but it is a great learning opportunity. This creates the opportunity to have the discussion about tagging photos. When I was in graduate school and we were taking pictures and posting them online, I asked my friends not to tag me in questionable photos or not to put them online, period. You don't want to be tagged in a photo that does not represent you in the best light.

We also take time to discuss who our "friends" are online. It is so easy to get caught up in how many likes and friends you have that you lose control. After this class discussion, some students comb through their accounts to make things private, evaluate their online relationships and delete photos. I encourage you to consider doing the same.

Challenge:
Look through your social media account –
would you hire yourself?

Emily Bach, a recent graduate in elementary education, says it best:

> Remember that you are YOU,
> regardless of what social platform
> you are on. Be a person of
> integrity in all of life, that way
> you don't ever have to worry
> about what people might "find
> out" about you. Take
> responsibility for your words and
> actions, both in real life and
> online. Once you've said it, you
> can't take it back. Each
> interaction you have with others
> is an opportunity!

This rings true in what you like, comment, reply, or share online...not just what you post. You represent yourself online in all that you do. Be sure that you are representing yourself in a professional way.

Other students find accurate hits online displaying awards, GPAs, or times on a track meet. These kinds of things don't show their professionalism, but they don't hurt, either. We use these examples to discuss how although we may find some things online are neutral, we want to make sure that we bolster our professional presence. We discuss some ways to do that by having an up-to-date digital portfolio, professional social media accounts, posting on educational blogs, etc.

Still, I have some students that don't find anything online about themselves, and they think that is a good thing. They are proud that they have locked down their digital presence for so long.

(Insert loud buzzer noise here) WRONG!

Maybe at one time, that was a good thing, but nowadays you want to be found online. If you aren't controlling your digital presence, then who is? That is a scary thought! Having nothing online about you is just as bad as an employer finding a picture of you holding a red Solo cup or playing a rousing game of flip cup while tailgating for the big game.

What do I mean by that, you may be asking? Well, when we see someone pictured with a red Solo cup, we have an assumption of what kind of liquid is in the cup, and it isn't Kool-Aid! Just like you don't want a future employer to find a picture of you with a questionable beverage in your hand, you don't want the future employer to search online and find a desert of nothingness out there. You want something to show up, and that something should be positive and professional.

Other times, students don't find anything about themselves online because they have a common name. If you are in this boat, then I suggest you start using your middle name or middle initial with your professional accounts. Use the same name on your resume, digital portfolio, and social media accounts. Then start creating amazing things under your professional name.

As we have mentioned, in addition to conducting background checks on a teacher candidate, many school districts will also Google you. They want to find you...they want to find out what you are doing, and what you have done to impact the lives of children. Use this as an opportunity to showcase yourself as a professional. You want to have a WOW digital presence, not a "meh" presence (Couros, 2016).

Former student and Colorado educator, Kaylee Strawhun shares, "my principal, who hired me with a team of teachers, told me he looked thoroughly through my personal website before hiring me. He claimed it made me stand out in huge ways and was another way the hiring team could get to know me."

Being a professional is not a light switch you turn on and off when you enter a classroom. I always tell my students to keep the professional public and the personal private. Megan VanKirk, a recent graduate in biology secondary education, shares this advice about her experience with the *"Google is the New Resume"* assignment:

I own my digital presence by
occasionally tweeting about
education strategies, science
teaching ideas, and encouraging
quotes on Twitter. Knowing that
my professional Twitter account
is public, I want to occasionally
update it to show future
employers my interest in having a
positive digital footprint. I will
also occasionally Google my
name, to check on my digital
presence. I will update security
settings if need be, to verify that
my personal accounts remain
personal!

I will even go as far as to delete
any accounts whose security
structure does not seem to truly
keep any personal information
private. Adding to a professional
Pinterest account occasionally is
another way that I work to own
my digital presence.

I hope that if future educators
were to look up my name online,
they would find multiple
professional social media
accounts demonstrating how
seriously I take the profession of
teaching, and my commitment to
a growth mindset!

Digital portfolios – your tool to rule them all

OK, I know that might be a little dramatic, but stick with me here. Teachers, administrators, and other education stakeholders want to see what you have been learning, sharing, and doing in the classroom. One way to showcase all your edu-awesomeness is by creating a digital portfolio.

Cue infomercial music here. Tired of lugging around a three-ring binder of notes, resources, lesson plans, folders, and worksheets? Is your binder full of ideas but you don't have anywhere to store them or organize them? Do you love your edu-collection of awesomeness but have no idea where anything is? Fear not! Start your digital portfolio and start it now! A digital portfolio is an online repository and centralized place to show off your edumagic!

The important thing to remember about a digital portfolio is that it is never complete – you can always keep learning, growing, and building. A digital portfolio has many magical powers and upgrades (Kappa Delta Pi, 2016):

✎ It provides a future employer with a visual representation of you. It highlights who you are, what you are all about, and why you want to teach...a one-stop spot for a future employer that they can refer to at a later date and time at their own convenience.

✎ It showcases your skills, strengths, field experiences, student teaching work, and work outside the classroom.

✎ It demonstrates your technical savvy – just by creating one.

There are so many free technology tools available for you to create a digital portfolio. I recommend that you find one that you like and use it. When searching for a technology tool, find something that is easy to use, has professional appeal, can be personalized to fit your unique self and is free (I tell my students that we teachers specialize in FREE). You may want to try Google Sites, Weebly, or Wix to create your digital portfolio.

Honestly, it really isn't about the tool but in how you use it to showcase your work and organize it. You want to make sure that your digital portfolio is easy to navigate. According to a webinar recorded by Kappa Delta Pi (2016), some foundational components that pre-service teachers include in their digital portfolios are: welcome, about me, contact, current resume, teaching philosophy, work samples, and more.

✎ The **welcome** page is the landing page for

your site. It welcomes viewers to your page and describes the purpose of the digital portfolio. It is a guide directing the viewer to what is found here.

🖊 The **about me** page is where you can get more personal with your content. Describe yourself as a person and as a teacher. Most pre-service teachers put their background, major and rationale for choosing it, graduation year, career goals, what they like doing in their spare time, interests, strengths, and other information. Consider adding fun facts about yourself to show some personality (this is where you can put in your secret talent that you play the ukulele)!

🖊 Your **professional resume** should include several categories (Snyder, 2018) such as contact information, education, student teaching and field experiences, work history, and teaching related experiences. Some additional (optional) categories include concise and clear objective, honors and awards, volunteer experience, professional memberships, and extracurricular activities. Snyder (2018) states that you must justify everything on your resume – it must be there for a reason. Be picky about what you showcase on your resume, as it should only be one page.

- The **contact page** is self-explanatory. Be sure to include your professional email, embed or provide a link to your professional Twitter and/or Pinterest feed, and link to a LinkedIn profile if you have one. In my opinion, please don't include your address or phone number– there are creepers out there.

- One of the most important features of a digital portfolio is your **work samples**! You want to include all the edu-awesome things that you are doing and learning, both in and out of the classroom! Be like a picky eater and only choose those materials that you are proud of and those that make you shine!

Remember how I said the digital portfolio is always growing, as it is a process and not a product? During your courses as you are completing assignments, consider adding them to your digital portfolio to showcase your learning – your future self will thank you.

Giulia Pucci, a freshman PreK-4 elementary education major, adds to her digital portfolio now, instead of waiting. She spices up her portfolio with nuggets of awesomeness. She really owned her digital presence by creating her digital portfolio to have her own personal look and feel. She customized pages and content by adding images, videos, and playlists. The style and artwork displayed on her site express who she is.

As you turn in an assignment for a class, ask yourself: *Is this something I would want a future employer to see?* If you can answer "YES" then put it in there! But don't just throw it in willy-nilly. Add some context around why you selected this piece, what you learned, how you can use it in your own classroom, etc. Make sure that you are always going back and growing your digital portfolio with lessons learned and new ideas.

Abbey Mae Method gives this advice to pre-service teachers:

> The digital portfolio is helpful as you prepare for interviews because it helps remind you of your proudest teacher moments that you want to talk about. I even used parts of my "teaching philosophy" page in some of the cover letters I wrote to the schools I applied to. It's an incredible resource that represents you, so use it!

I would like to sum up this chapter by sharing this advice from pre-service teacher, Kaitlin Gionta, secondary English major:

Your digital presence is a reflection of your work in the classroom and what you have retained. Don't be afraid to share what you know, get involved in the online community, tweet out your portfolio, etc.! These are things that you will put so much time and energy into that you should be confident in the final product; however, it's important that while you are confident you stay humble.

You are involved in a community of constant learners, and no one is overarchingly better than anyone else. There are going to be things that you can teach to others, but there are also going to be things that you can learn from others, and that's what is so beautiful about the online community.

So, Now What?

- ✏ Create a digital portfolio now! It is never too early or too late to start.
- ✏ If you already have a digital portfolio collecting dust, blow some dust off it, jazz it up and make it sparkle. Add in assignments that you are proud to showcase.
- ✏ Get it out there: Link your digital portfolio to your professional social media accounts (Twitter, Pinterest, Instagram, LinkedIn). Also, consider adding a link to your digital portfolio to your resume via QR code. Spread the word!
- ✏ Already have a digital portfolio that you created for a class? Then update it. Change the words to present tense. Update it from an academic and student perspective to a professional perspective – you are a professional, time to make your digital resume sound like it.
- ✏ Don't just let it sit online – use it. For instance, when you are asked by a future employer how you managed a classroom or what ideas you have to integrate technology, pull out your digital portfolio and show an example!
- ✏ Google yourself often – you want to

---

know what is out there about you.

U – Unite your PLN

"The important thing is that we stick together!"
– Buzz Lightyear, Toy Story

Just like Buzz Lightyear had his friends in Andy's room, one thing every teacher needs in their basket of educational goodies is understanding of the power of a personalized learning network (PLN). I am sure you have heard the phrase professional or personal learning network (PLN). Just for clarity's sake, I will be using the definition of a PLN identified by Whitby (2013), "personalized learning network," meaning that you are a professional learner and a personal learner. Whitby continues identifying a PLN as "a tool that uses social media and technology to collect, communicate, collaborate and create with connected colleagues anywhere at any time."

Hannah Turk came into the meeting room with her laptop and announced to the small group of students who were present for the introduction meeting to our online class, "if you get me to like Twitter that would be a miracle."

I remember sarcastically thinking to myself, "Oh wonderful! This is a great way to start the class meeting."

Students looked at me with shock and a little bit of disbelief that Hannah would come in and say something like that to a professor. I then channeled my inner Barney Stinson, from *How I Met Your Mother* (2005), and said,

"Challenge accepted." That seemed to break the ice. Everyone relaxed, and the introduction meeting went smoothly. Little did I know what was going to happen when Hannah got connected to her PLN.

You see, in the class, students are required to build a PLN. This usually is greeted with eye rolls and snickering by students. It's OK. I have come to accept it.

Maybe you had heard of a PLN before and thought to yourself, "I won't need that until I have my first teaching job." That is what a lot of students think. Well, that and the following (not an exhaustive list):

- 🪄 I don't have anything to say...I'm not even a teacher yet.
- 🪄 No one will follow me.
- 🪄 Nobody cares what I have to say.

Well, you are WRONG! (*Insert loud buzzer noise here.*)

First, of course you have something to say – everyone does! Did you know that administrators are looking to new educators for innovative teaching techniques and technology tools? Tweet out what you are learning in class with relative hashtags, and you will get some responses. Don't tweet out answers to a quiz or a test of course, but think of one takeaway from a class and tweet it out. Other educators love to read about what you are learning. Specifically, people want to read about your take on the learning. What do you think about this technique? Tool? Strategy? Have you observed it in a field experience or in student teaching placement? Have you read some research or an article about it? Have you discussed this concept in a class? It is great to quote a tweet and add your two cents to it, giving the reader a glimpse into what you thought of when you read the tweet.

It is so important to be you online – remember that whole chapter on digital presence? Embrace your professional persona and be authentic. Having a PLN is all about engaging in the professional world and building and growing together; not having canned answers and takeaways from class because a professor told you to tweet, but to really taking ownership of your learning and putting yourself out there. You can also tweet out a question to one of your PLN power players, and you will get a reply.

Abbey Mae Method was leading a class discussion during her trends and issues in education class about service learning. She remembered that in the course "Technology of Instruction" we had a guest speaker join us via Skype to talk about service learning. She logged onto Twitter and contacted Mike Soskil, the 2016 Pennsylvania Teacher of the Year and an amazing educator who has done many great projects with his students.

As a class, we were honored enough to have Mike join us via Skype and talk about his experience and service learning project for his students. By being a connected pre-service teacher, Abbey Mae was able to reach out to him, interview him, and bring in his expertise into her discussion with her peers. Here is her story about the experience in her own words:

The inspiration for this paper
came from a guest speaker we
had in Technology of Instruction
class, Mike Soskil, who did a
service learning project with his
class.

Hoping to gain some practical
advice for my paper, I tweeted
Mr. Soskil and asked to do a
Skype interview. He
enthusiastically agreed. The
interview was such a wonderful
and helpful experience.

Mr. Soskil provided very
insightful advice on how to create
a classroom culture that embraces
the creative thinking needed to
run an effective service-learning
project. His personal stories
added vividness and clarity to all
his information and suggestions.

Most of all, it was hugely
encouraging to talk to someone
who had successfully
implemented both an
exploratory, self-motivated
classroom culture and successful
service learning projects.

This connection would have been
impossible without the resources
available through Twitter.

How powerful is that? Think about that: she had a
Teacher of the Year award winner and service learning
guru available to chat with her! She was able to bring in
first-hand experience with service learning. All of that
happened just because she joined Twitter and really
jumped in with both feet.

Challenge:

Get connected on Twitter.

Find people who will inform your education, speak
into your life and help you grow as an educator. Get
connected now; it is never too early or too late.

Don't collect followers like *Pokémon* but engage
and grow with your followers and those you are
following. Some pre-service teachers worry about how
many followers they have. I like to tell them it's not about
how many followers you have, it's about the quality and
the conversation that you are having. Engage them in
conversation by asking questions and replying to posts.

Sharing is caring, so share out your favorite
techniques, strategies, and tools. Just as we like to read
our favorite blog and website updates, people want to see
your Twitter updated. I am not saying post every hour on
the hour, but use tools like Tweetdeck or Hootsuite to
schedule out tweets daily, weekly, or monthly. Seriously,
Hootsuite is my Twitter lifesaver. With Hootsuite, I

schedule posts to go out on Facebook, Twitter, and Insta each day. All in one click of a button, I have posted content to three different social media outlets to reach my audience where they are. I can customize content for each network and sometimes I do just that using hashtags.

Another feature of Hootsuite is that I can focus on the hashtags that mean the most to me. So obviously, I have #gccedu (the education department hashtag) and #edumagic (this book's official hashtag) up so I can see the content being posted there.

But, I don't have to stop at just hashtags. I have some of my edu-rockstars' profiles up too so I can keep up-to-date posts about what they are saying. You can do so much with Hootsuite – it is a powerful T3 (teacher Twitter timesaver). I encourage you to check it out. And oh, did I mention it is FREE?

Whitby (2013) suggests spending twenty minutes a day engaged with your PLN. This is a great way to keep your feed fresh and helps you with those time management skills. We are all busy. Again, it's not about how many followers you have; it's about the quality of your content.

Another neat way to join in on the Twitter conversation is to share what you are doing and learning in classes. For instance, if you are preparing for a lesson you can sell tickets for (Burgess, 2012) or rearranging the classroom to facilitate a discussion, take a picture of it and post it on Twitter with some related hashtags and a short blurb about it.

Another interesting way to use Twitter is to tweet out notes. Instead of keeping a document of notes during a conference, I use Twitter to share what I am learning so it can be shared with the world. I encourage you to do the same. For example, Emily Bach, a recent graduate, shares that she attended an edcamp and "tweeted out a thought about being mindful as teachers and regulating ourselves, and hundreds of other edu-awesome teachers liked and retweeted it!"

Maybe your school or education department has a hashtag – use it and share what you are learning in classes. Does your school or department not have a hashtag yet? There is no time like the present to create one. Just a few tips before you get started:

- Google or search your hashtag first if you are making it up. Seriously do that – you don't want to find out that the hashtag you have been using for your school is associated with something weird. Make sure it isn't being used for another company or organization.
- Make it short but memorable – you don't want it to take up too much character space.
- Relate it to your topic or area. For example, our education department's hashtag is #gccedu for Grove City College, Department of Education.
- Have a couple of ideas that fit these criteria? Put it to a vote with the class or department – best hashtag wins!

🖋 Consider having a hashtag for a campus event, organization, educational club, or guest speaker to keep the conversation going.

Hannah Turk's story, just like yours, it isn't finished. She spent that summer working through a framework for teaching and infusing technology tools where it was appropriate. At the end of the summer, Hannah had a digital portfolio to showcase her work, a few boards on Pinterest, and tweets out there under her professional Twitter handle. She came back to campus in the fall, continued to lurk around Twitter, and would occasionally tweet a few ideas.

Something happened to Hannah during that time when she was no longer required to tweet or have a PLN for class: she got it. She saw the power of Twitter and was connected to people in the state, country, and worldwide. Hannah went from connecting with a few pre-service teachers and peers to connecting with educators, administrators, education organizations, and school districts. She went from not really liking Twitter to leading workshops at the college and at state level conferences about the power of a PLN. She even co-led a webinar about the power of a PLN for an international educational honorary!

Hannah knew that after graduation she would be moving to a different state, so she followed that state's educational hashtag. From that hashtag, she related to educators and administrators from that specific area. Her PLN helped to connect her for multiple job interviews in the area she was looking to move to. She received job offers from all those interviews...she had her choice of jobs as a new teacher graduate! Let me repeat that – a college graduate had her pick of jobs. Powerful stuff, people! Your PLN is a force to be reckoned with – use it wisely.

But that's not all (yeah, I know I sound like an infomercial here); Hannah has enjoyed networking on Twitter so much that she is even a Twitter chat co-moderator for an international chat called #nt2t! It is an online chat for teachers who are new to Twitter, and she is an amazing voice and mentor in that chat. If you are up on a Saturday morning (9:00 AM ET) join in on the conversation.

For some pre-service teachers, social media and connecting come very naturally. One such student is Richard J. (RJ) Dula, math and history major. He expressed these thoughts on being a connected pre-service teacher:

> When I first started classes, I
> never thought that my skills with
> social media beforehand would
> be so helpful to me when using a
> professional Twitter and building
> a PLN. The impact of Twitter
> and a PLN on me is that I have
> realized that I have a voice, a
> bunch of ideas, and the hunger to
> make a change.

> Get involved but don't get
> discouraged at first.
>
> It takes a while for you to build a
> PLN and connections with
> teachers that like, comment,
> retweet, and read your tweets and
> blog posts. Just keep being
> involved and find your niche.
>
> For me, I would say my niche is
> social media; for others, it may be
> writing blog posts on ed books.
> Some like doing write-ups about
> different tech tools, etc. Whatever
> it is, find your niche and stick to
> it. Eventually, people will notice,
> and it will be all worthwhile.

One way to build your PLN and to own your learning is by attending conferences. You need to attend at least one conference or professional development event during your college career. If you don't do anything else, just attend.

But don't attend for a grade or extra credit in a class. Go for the love of learning. I want you to take some time and think about what are some areas in which you need to grow as an educator? Is there a strategy or tool that you need to become more familiar with? Go ahead, write it down. I'll wait.

Now unleash the power of Google and find a conference or professional development workshop that focuses on that area of need. No luck? Seek out webinars or book studies on the topic. Dig around and find something that is going to help you grow and learn as an educator. If you are feeling chatty, ask a professor or mentor to see which professional development events s/he attends.

By attending conferences and other professional development events, you will meet people who are involved with Twitter, so connect with them in person and then follow them on Twitter. Or maybe you're in a session and want to tweet takeaways from the topic; what you can do is tag the person and use the event's hashtag in the tweet (don't tweet 100 things but maybe a few tweets). By doing this, you are showing the speaker you care, you are talking about things that maybe other people missed because they were in a different session, and you are opening it up to people across all the country or the world!

One last thing I always tell people is that you don't have to follow everybody. Be picky about who you follow – just because someone follows you doesn't mean you have to follow him/her back. Check out their feed see if it is of interest to you and if it is going to help you grow.

Favorite PLN Moments

I can't end this chapter without giving a few examples of powerful PLN moments. Pre-service teachers have had authors retweet their posts or comment on their work. One story is from a former student who was a fantastic teaching assistant, Derek Witmer. Derek is a second-grade educator in eastern Pennsylvania, where he shares his passion for educational technology and STEM in his classroom by challenging students to find solutions to everyday problems using critical thinking skills and collaboration. One cold January morning, he was teaching his second graders about air resistance. To make this topic tangible students created and tested out parachutes. To his surprise, the Pennsylvania Secretary of Education came into his classroom to observe this activity. During the activity, Derek tweeted pictures and comments, and the Secretary of Education liked the tweets. Later pictures of his classroom were on the Pennsylvania Department of Education website. Derek was in awe, and so proud of his students and their hard work!

Emily Bach shares that at first, she was a little skeptical about using Twitter to connect but has grown to enjoy it. Because of her use of Twitter, she has connected with practicing educators, organizations, and administrators. She has learned about potential job offers and educational opportunities that speak to her specific interests in Spanish education.

Anna Emmons had a similar experience when she recounts her first experience with Twitter:

> I was hesitant about the idea of using Twitter for educational purposes at first. Full disclosure, I was incredibly not excited to have to use it.

But being able to connect and network with so many experienced social studies teachers who are all doing such great things in their classrooms is an incredible gift. Learning how Twitter chats work, interacting with experienced teachers and learning from what they have to offer, and being able to share my thoughts and get feedback were all great things I got (and am continuing to get) from that experience.

Twitter Chats

A PLN is so much more than a professional outlet for you – it is a way for you to grow, learn, encourage, and support others in the field. It helps you to gain support and to support others. One way to do this is by participating in an educational Twitter chat. You may be asking yourself, "What are Twitter chats?" Twitter chats are education-related chats that occur daily throughout the year (Ward, 2017). Chats are related to a specific educational topic with related questions. For example, some are related to formative assessment or a specific technology tool. Chats range from 15 minutes to an hour in length and are very informal when it comes to jumping in when you can (or leaving when you need to).

The first step in joining a Twitter chat is by first

searching to see when chats are happening. You can search Cybraryman's Google Site (Blumengarten, n.d.) to find a chat on a specific day and time or you can search Participate (n.d.) to find a chat that is happening today!

Once you find a chat to participate in, the next step is to set up your Tweetdeck or Hootsuite account with the specific chat hashtag. From there, tune in on the specific date and time of the chat (double check time zones) with a cup of coffee and get ready for an experience. I sometimes encourage my students to hang out with a friend to do a few chats together that way they can learn from each other and keep each other on pace. I require my students to participate in 5 Twitter chats each semester. Maybe you are like my students – a little nervous before their first chat; that is OK. You are allowed to be because it is likely something new. But, please try to embrace it and go with the flow.

Kylee McLafferty, a freshman PreK-4 and special education major, shares about an experience that she had while connecting with a practicing teacher during a Twitter chat.

> One of the teachers in the chat was so impressed that a pre-service teacher was using Twitter that he direct messaged me afterward to reach out and say that if I ever needed anything he would be more than happy to help.

We continue to like and comment
on each other's tweets, and he
answers any questions that I
have.

Abby Ross, an English secondary and
communication major shares this story from a Twitter
chat that she participated in:

I was participating in the
#NoVaedchat and met someone
who taught in my home county.
We connected, and I learned that
she was a Grove City College
graduate, where I was attending
school.

She attended Edcamp GCC, and
we were able to meet in person
and continue the collaboration
we were having online, in person.

RJ Dula shares this advice about Twitter chats:

I realized from all the different
Twitter education chats and
interactions with other teachers
out there that I can make a
difference.

Sometimes people are so scared of Twitter education chats; they often think to themselves, "what will they think of me? What if I say something wrong? What if I have no idea what they are talking about? What if I have never experienced that?"

I think that once I realized I can find a way to contribute to every point with experiences from when I was in school, or thoughts from a lecture in class, or even an idea, that I truly fell in love with the Twitter chats and went for it.

The cool thing that I realized is that people are watching and reading what you say. I was participating in a DITCH that Textbook Twitter chat and the author of the book retweeted something I said and replied to it. I was thinking to myself "OMG! THE Matt Miller just retweeted something I said and replied to it!" Not only that but we connected even more throughout the chat, and he EVEN sent me an autographed copy of his book.

It is moments like these that are funny, but also validated my journey towards becoming a teacher. I realized that I am on the right path and that my ideas do matter. I want to make a difference in whatever way that I can, and my experiences from Twitter validated that.

Twitter chat best practices

- Follow the moderator of the chat. This is the person who is posting the questions. You want to make sure you are following him or her, so you don't miss a question.
- Answer the questions as the moderator posts them. Do NOT be that person who answers all the questions in advance and then leaves the chat – not cool. Now, I am not saying don't schedule your responses to questions using a tool like Tweetdeck. By all means, go for it. In fact, if you can, it is encouraged so you can focus on conversation with others. What I am saying is, if the moderator posts all the questions in the chat at the beginning, don't answer each question in one tweet with the hashtag two minutes after that chat has started, wash your hands of it, and go get a pizza. By doing that you are only cheating yourself of learning and

connecting with others. You are just answering five or so questions and not really contributing much to the conversation. Don't be like that.

- Don't feel like you have to answer every question posted.
- Follow along with the question and answer format. For example, when the moderator posts question one, you will see Q1 and the question to follow. Craft your response with A1 (for answer one) and post your response.
- Engage others in conversation about the topic – don't be afraid to ask questions, share ideas, and have a side conversation during the chat. Sometimes those side conversations are the most beneficial.
- Be professional – enough said.
- Use this time to build that positive, professional digital presence.

So, now what?

- 🪄 Start early, start now! It's never too early. What does this look like? Get a Twitter handle that is professional and creative. Some students use a combination of first initial, last name. My favorite one so far is @simply_RJD, RJ Dula who we heard from before. He really lives and breathes his mantra: "#Student TODAY, #Teacher TOMORROW, #Learner ALWAYS."

- 🪄 Another thing to think about when creating your Twitter profile is to select a professional picture. Now I don't mean senior picture-level photos or a random selfie. Instead, choose something in between that shows your professional side and some personality.

- 🪄 Your bio is so important, as it really shows who you are and is your digital handshake to people. Most pre-service teachers put their year, major, etc. but don't be afraid to jazz it up. Add a favorite educational quote or some fun facts about you.

- 🪄 Brand yourself as a professional educator (spoiler alert: you are one). Remember everyone has a voice and something to share. Tweet out what you are learning or a lesson you are doing in class. Join a Twitter chat or two, or three! The more you know, the more you grow. Share what you are learning. Why? Because sharing is caring!

- Your bio is so important, as it really shows who you are and is your digital handshake to people. Most pre-service teachers put their year, major, etc. but don't be afraid to jazz it up. Add a favorite educational quote or some fun facts about you.

- Brand yourself as a professional educator (spoiler alert: you are one). Remember everyone has a voice and something to share. Tweet out what you are learning or a lesson you are doing in class. Maybe you prepared some great handouts or manipulatives for class. Tweet out a pic and how you are using it in your field or student teaching.

- Join a Twitter chat or two, or three! The more you know, the more you grow. Share what you are learning. Why? Because sharing is caring!

M – Megapixels

"All you need is a little faith, trust, and pixie dust."
– Peter Pan

Megapixels are what my dad calls sprinkles – add sprinkles to your assignments to jazz it up a bit. Let me share with you a story from Emily Wilson, a recent graduate in the field of Pre-K-4 elementary education. Since her freshman year, Emily has been developing herself as a professional, attending workshops and edcamps around the area. She learned about *Breakout EDU* during her professional travels and decided to implement it into her student teaching placement. In case you are not familiar with *Breakout EDU*, it basically takes the idea of an escape room and puts it into a box. Participants are required to implement critical thinking skills, logic, communication, and collaboration skills to solve puzzles and work together to break out of the room (or in this case break into a box in the classroom).

Emily was a student teacher in a math lab setting where students solved math problems in creative ways, explaining their thinking behind the process. In this class, solving math problems is not just about the answer but how you get there. She decided to create a *Breakout EDU* activity where students had to solve math problems to crack codes and open locks. The weekend before her lesson, Emily was preparing official spy folders, codes with invisible ink, ciphers, and clues. She had no idea what to expect when she came in Monday morning to teach her lesson. Would the clues be too hard? Would the students just give up and put their heads down? Would they be engaged and want to try more?

She set up a story where students had to solve math problems to get into a backup box of food for a penguin, just in case the zookeeper didn't get back in time. Emily passed out official folders, complete with challenges and clues, pens, and UV flashlights, and the clock was set. Students worked in small groups to solve math problems with regrouping. They were excited to use their math skills to crack codes and use invisible ink to get the lock to open. At the end of the lesson, students solved 18 subtraction problems without even noticing! How cool is that? I don't know about you, but I can't remember a time when solving 18 math problems was so much fun.

Challenge:
"Think outside the bun" when it comes to lesson planning.

Megan Vankirk recounts a lesson from her student teaching experience about the cell cycle, where she added movement. She wanted to give her ninth-grade students in her general biology class a completely different way of learning.

Megan planned a lesson in which she designed a station activity where students themselves became cells and moved through cell cycle stations. At each station, the students would document what happened to them at that particular phase, then color their cell correspondingly. By the end of the cycle, students understood what happened to a cell during each phase. This required a lot of preparation time on Megan's part. She designed a notes packet from scratch, where the notes for each phase were on the back of a picture of a cell. She created the instructions for each station, telling students what to take notes on, and what to color on the corresponding cell.

Finally, she had to set up materials at each station, along with a timer on the board that allowed students to flow through the stations in a time-effective manner, to complete the cycle in one class period. Though this took a lot of planning beforehand, students had full notes on the cell cycle, along with pictures and notecards they could make from their note packet to use in following classes and in their own studying. This was so much more interesting than lecturing on the cycle of a cell. Students got to experience it first-hand; now that's adding in some *edumagic*!

During her student teaching placement, middle-level major, Katy Gibson had students write exit tweets. This is an interesting story because she used a tool that students were already familiar with, but using it in an analog way. Instead of students tweeting live exit tweets, she had them complete exit tickets that followed the format of Twitter, but on paper. She collected them after the lesson and posted them on the bulletin board in the classroom. It was a neat way for students to connect with Katy after a lesson and for them to continue to learn. Some students used their slips of paper to ask a question, post a response, or tell a joke or fun science fact. For example, one student's Twitter slip read, "Where does a mimicking bird live? @mermaidlover75 #birdsounds #caralaram." She posted a picture of this Twitter slip and, in her comment, replied that they mostly live in Australia.

What I liked most about this lesson is that Katy would take a picture of the Twitter slip and post a reply. This lesson was a great way for students to continue their curiosity in learning the new topics. She continues to do this activity in her seventh-grade math class in Virginia, where students tweet out their thoughts and questions about math-related topics. By doing so, she is able to get a beat on their learning and reply to their questions using a tool that they are already familiar with – even if it isn't digital.

I encourage you to teach lessons using tools that students are already familiar with. Reach them where they are with what they use. So, which tool are my students currently obsessed with? *Snapchat.* You guys, I still don't really "get" *Snapchat,* but I will tell you who does, Tara Martin, a "*REAL*ly" amazing educator.

With a simple Google search, I typed in "Snapchat" and "education," and one of the results was Tara Martin's video from ISTE 2017 (Martin, 2017). I watched it and was amazed and inspired by how she embraced a new tool for educational good. This was all born out of the idea that her son was using Snapchat to connect with his friends. She used Snapchat to make #booksnaps. Not familiar with #booksnaps? She took the idea of using text, having students take a picture, and annotation to make visual connections. Just recently I had students use *Snapchat* to create #istesnaps (a cousin, in my opinion to a #booksnap) about the ISTE Standards for Educators and Students (2017). Students chose standards, and they created an #istesnap that they posted on social media showing their annotations to make the text more relatable through *Bitmojis,* gifs, annotations, text, and graphics.

Challenge:
Find out and use the technology tools that your students are using.

My friends, I challenge you to do the same. Now, please know that I have zero experience with *Snapchat*, but my students know that app and use it daily. I wanted to reach them using a tool that they already use. They enjoyed the lesson and could make connections to the text in a different way. Which technology tool are your students using daily? Maybe you don't know which tool they are currently obsessed with – so then my challenge to you is to ask! Ask them, seriously. Yeah, they may look at you with a confused expression on their face; they may laugh, or they may take a long pause – but ask and engage them in conversation. Next, ask yourself, *how can I use it in my class to reach them?* Then do it!

So, now what?

- Get outside the box and try out a new teaching strategy or technique.
- I like to move it, move it! Don't be afraid to add movement to your lesson.
- Reach your students using relevant tools.

A – Always Be...

"Be prepared" – Scar, Lion King

Always be prepared to be approached at a conference

When pre-service teachers attend a conference with me, they are always surprised that they are approached by a practicing teacher and asked questions about who they are and where they teach. So, be prepared for it. Be prepared to have an elevator pitch ready about who you are and what you do beyond your name, major, and where you go to school. Share why you are attending the conference or what you are presenting about. Ask the teacher about his or her career and actively listen. Don't just have a one-sided conversation, but ask genuine questions.

You never know where a conversation can lead. I had one student who ordered business cards because she was attending so many conferences. She even used them during her job search at career fairs. On her business card, she included a link to her professional website and how to contact her via Twitter. You never know where a new connection and follow up can lead – in some cases, conversations lead to job advice and interviews!

Always be prepared with technology

As an edtech professor, I always say to my

students that tech is great when it works. My advice to you is that when it comes to technology, make sure that you try it out first. By trying it out first, you can avoid the possibility of having to update flash players or a whole computer update! Also, try it out in the classroom. You don't want to find out the day of your lesson that the video that you wanted to show to your students is on YouTube and that it is blocked.

You can also make sure that your internet connection is good to go and that your ad blocker is on. You need to have a backup plan just in case the internet goes down. I know it may not happen, but be prepared and have a backup activity for students to do. This happened to me just recently with the STEM DAY event (referenced in the previous chapter). In one of our stations, we had students using virtual reality headsets, but we got to the school and realized that the students were not allowed to bring their phones to class. So, we planned a backup activity where students would use a *Nearpod* teacher-guided lesson to explore Mars. We had all the computers set up and ready to roll, but then found that the flash player needed to be updated.

So, we had to go to plan C, which was to check out a virtual tour of the Smithsonian where students were able to explore different exhibits. So that lesson went from plan A, to plan B, to plan C. Yes, we did have some students who were disappointed in not using the headsets, but they still were able to have a virtual reality experience.

When using technology, be prepared by having websites you want to visit pulled up on tabs first, so you don't have to search for them during the lesson. It can be a little nerve-wracking while teaching if you are trying to search for a website. You can use tools like extensions such as <u>OneTab</u>. OneTab will save all of the tabs you want to use into one list, so you don't have to search through everything (you can even share out the link to the tab, so everyone is on the same page – literally!).

Be prepared with tech by keeping track of the time. It is a good practice while teaching any lesson that you keep track of your timing and pacing. One tool that I use is <u>Classroom Screen</u>. Don't be like me and tell students, "Ok you have three minutes to think, pair, share," but really only give them two minutes. By using Classroom Screen, I can easily keep a timer up on the board, so we know how much time is left for the activity. I can not only set a timer, but I can also use a random name generator, insert QR code for a link to a site (or OneTab) I want my students to use during class, text block with a welcome message or some Monday motivational quote, and much more.

Sometimes even with all of your planning, things can still go wrong. Tom Miller, a recent graduate in PreK-4, shared his experience with lessons learned and the importance of having a team. Here is his story:

> My pre-professional experiences
> in the classroom were the most
> formative moments of my
> academic career.

I collected a wealth of strategies, knowledge, and wisdom from my cooperating teachers and my students. Through all of that, I discovered that taking bold and calculated risks was the key to a successful and student-centered learning environment.

During my student teaching, I decided to literally aim for the stars and transform my classroom and an entire day of academics into Star Wars in honor of May the Fourth. It was a lofty goal and one that I wasn't entirely qualified for (creative decorations and Pinterest-worthy transformational lessons are not my forte). However, I used my passion for the science fiction franchise and my desire to wow my kids to fuel my efforts. My co-op was thrilled for the opportunity and encouraged me to take as many risks as I saw fit to pull this off.

I started brainstorming. I had my
students color and cut stars
during the whole week leading up
to the final show while keeping
the purpose of the stars a secret to
everyone. I prepped Math and
Reading centers to reflect Star
Wars. I created a multi-tiered
behavior management plan that
was motivating and exciting to
both me and the students, using
Star Wars character cards and a
planetary "Race to Save the
Galaxy" poster. I bought a Han
Solo costume to wear for the
whole day. I handpicked the
soundtrack that would play all
day. I recruited other staff
members to help me plan and set
up. I plotted how I was going to
meticulously set up everything
early in the morning. It was
coming together wonderfully.

Then I woke up late on Friday. In
a panic, I arrived at the school in
a sloppy Han Solo costume and
an untransformed classroom.

Fortunately, if there was one
thing I learned while student
teaching, it was to roll with the
punches. And so, we did. The
kids didn't know a thing.

We sent them off to gym class
and then went into tornado mode
to transform the classroom. An
idea, teamwork, a little bit of
prep, a little less skill in crafts and
arts, and whole lot of passion led
to the most magical smiles and
reactions from second graders I
could have ever dreamed. We
had a blast, and we learned a lot
too that day. But above all, I'm
thankful my co-op encouraged
me to follow my dream and take
a leap. I'm encouraged that
teachers really can do anything
they set their minds to, especially
when it's for the kids. I'm excited
to take risks and use my passions
to fuel my future classroom.

This just goes to show although things may not go
according to plan, if your focus remains the students –
you are on the right track. You don't have to go big or go
home with lessons; sometimes it is just as simple as
reaching your students where they are at and using tools
that are relevant to their lives.

So, now what?

> 🪄 Use technology for a purpose – it is not just one more thing. We don't just show our students something shiny and new and throw it into our curriculum willie-nillie. I mean we could, but we may not be successful. Instead, we must integrate it with meaning behind it and curriculum tied to it.
> 🪄 Always have a plan B or C, or maybe even Z!

Always be an advocate

During our teaching day, we wear many hats. Sometimes we put on the nurse hat, or the therapist hat, or the parent hat. At times we may need to try on the advocate hat for our students. During your college career, you may have to advocate for yourself. Giulia Pucci, shares about an experience where she had to advocate for herself to get a valuable learning experience.

> I've been really interested in testing to get certified in Music Education, so I wanted to try observing in a music classroom to see how it feels.

Our field experiences don't
advertise that we're allowed to
observe in classrooms outside of
our certifications, but my field
adviser said that we had some
wiggle room in our learning. I
spoke up and got permission to
explore Music Education – I
loved it!

It is important to speak up for yourself and ask questions. You may be surprised at the response.

Sometimes you must be your own advocate in the world of teaching and learning. It can be difficult to advocate for yourself during student teaching, but Emily Bach did just that when she was uncertain of co-op expectations. She shares this story:

In one of my student teaching
placements, I was very confused
by the expectations my
cooperating teacher had for me.
Instead of just trying to get by, I
sat down with her one afternoon
and asked if we could meet each
week for her to give me a brief
vision of what she was looking
for. Even though those meetings
only happened a few times, I did
something about my discomfort
and confusion by talking to my
co-op face to face.

A conversation now could provide a world of difference. Don't be afraid to share your thoughts and feelings whether that be with a cooperating teacher, field supervisor, or a professor. Sometimes just having a conversation in person can help with understanding the purpose and expectations behind an assignment or activity.

Challenge:
Be a voice for your own learning. If you don't, who will?

For many, student teaching is a time where a student feels that they need to prove themselves worthy for the field of education. You may feel that some things are insurmountable, like defeating a giant. Try something new and don't be afraid to fail even if it doesn't turn out just right you are still learning.

Megan VanKirk shares this story about her student teaching placements and how she had to advocate for herself:

> I had to advocate for myself when
> first starting out as a student
> teacher in both of my placements.

Most student teacher co-ops have seen a wide variety of student teachers come through their classrooms, and thus do not know the teaching level of their student teacher at their first meeting. The co-ops I taught alongside seemed to wait to see my confidence level amongst their students before throwing me into consistent teaching. To gain their trust, I would ask questions about what my co-op was doing, what they loved about teaching, how they worked to engage students, how they wrote tests, etc. and learned so much through simply observing. In doing each of these things, I found that I was advocating for myself as a pre-service teacher and slowly gained not only the trust, but also the friendship of my co-ops.

During the first few days of her student teaching placement, Megan took an active role in the classroom. From day one, she would rarely just be sitting in the back of the room – she would be interacting with students, engaging with the content, and learning from her cooperating teacher. It is important to show others that you are willing to do what it takes to make an impact on the lives of students.

So, now what?

- ✏ Have conversations and ask questions. Genuinely learn from others.
- ✏ If you don't understand something, ASK! There is never a dumb question, only questions that don't get asked.

Always be a professional

When you are in the classroom, you are a professional, a role model to students, so embrace it. Own it! Dress to impress. Don't pull out that wrinkly pair of khakis that need to be ironed and head out the door. Take time to make yourself look good. Don't be like the evil queen and stand in front of your mirror asking, "who is the fairest in all of the land," but you want to make yourself presentable and professional. Not only be professional in your dress, but if you are going to talk the talk, you have to walk the walk.

This means communicating professionally in face-to-face meetings, emails, and written work. Always address (unless told otherwise) your cooperating teacher (and professors for that matter) with Mr., Mrs., or Dr. and then their last name. Don't just call them by their last name (ugh!) – it reminds me of a football coach calling a player off the field, "Hey Johnson, nice work!"

When you are writing an email to your cooperating teacher (and professors), always start with a greeting (for example, *"Hi Mrs. Johnson, I hope that you are doing well"*). Don't just go right into your email. Also, end your email with your name.

I know it is simple, but please double-check your spelling and grammar. When it comes to written work, double- and triple-check. I once had a student who pulled a resource from Pinterest and printed it out (nothing wrong with that, yet...) and gave it to her students studying Spanish. She later found that the worksheet she gave the students had words misspelled and conjugated incorrectly. You don't want to teach the students something wrong and have to reteach it because you didn't vet your resource! That is why before you print or use a resource with your students read it over, and check for credibility. Be a good digital citizen, just like you want your students to be.

So, now what?

- 🪄 Dress to impress.
- 🪄 Talk the talk and walk the walk.
- 🪄 Check out your resources BEFORE you use them.

Always be ok with making a mistake

You will always be learning throughout life. Realize it now. Remember that learning isn't always reflected in a grade like an A+, sometimes learning takes the form of failing. You may fail a quiz, a test, or a final. You may hit a roadblock or a bump in the road. It is OK...take a deep a breath and accept it. But, that grade or failure does not define you. We are human, we will fail, but it is about how we get back up from that failure that defines us. When failure happens, channel your inner Dory from *Finding Nemo* (Stanton, Unkrich, Brooks, DeGeneres, & Gould, 2013) and "just keep swimming." That is exactly what Abbey Mae Method did. She shares an experience that she had during a field experience:

> I completed two of my field experiences at a school near my hometown. Although not required by the assignment, I wanted to challenge myself to do a field in a setting where I would be really stretched.
>
> For one of these field experiences, my cooperating teacher was absent for one of the days that I was observing, so I became the interim substitute because I was familiar with the labs the students were doing while the actual substitute present was not. This was the most challenging day of teaching I have ever experienced. The classes were extremely difficult to handle, as I did not know the students and had virtually no authority over them as a field student.

In fact, Abbey Mae and the substitute teacher had to call security to keep the students in the classroom. It would have been easy for her to leave that class feeling defeated, that she had failed. Think about it, the students didn't listen and were out of control. She could have left never wanting to go into a similar school again, based on that one experience. But no! Abbey Mae did not let it get her down. Instead, she left wanting more and energized to learn from that experience. She goes on to share:

> All I wanted was to go back and figure out a way to motivate the students to take an interest in the lab and to respect me as a person. This experience expanded my heart for schools in underserved communities and gave me a valuable perspective on some of the challenges faced by these communities and schools.

Today, Abbey Mae has just been hired at a charter school in Pittsburgh, PA where she will be working with middle school students in the area of science. Abbey Mae demonstrated growth mindset during her experience by embracing and learning from this difficulty.

Growth mindset is a topic I teach about in my class during the first week. Let's take some time to unpack this term a little bit. According to Dweck (2014, p. 10), there are two types of mindsets: fixed and growth, "In a fixed mindset, people believe that basic talents and abilities are fixed traits. However, in a growth mindset, people believe that basic abilities can be developed through hard work, good strategies, and good mentoring."

How can having a growth mindset help you with being a pre-service teacher? Well just by its very nature a growth mindset is laser-locked on learning. Dweck states that students with a growth mindset apply themselves by putting in an effort to complete a task, stick to tasks that are challenging, learn from their mistakes through reflection, and they also show resilience (p.10).

An important feature of the growth mindset is reflection. Each semester, I try something new in my class. This past year I tried out a technology tool called GooseChase. Students used this app to participate in a scavenger hunt around campus. I did this activity during the first week of class for two reasons: as a team building activity and for students to become more familiar with the campus.

I teach two sections of the class back-to-back, and during the 8 A.M. class the activity went off without a hitch. Students were posting pictures, adding comments, and running around campus completing missions. When students finished, they came back to the class, and we discussed ways to use this app in their future classrooms with their students.

I was excited to show the next section this cool app. I sent them out in teams with the code and thought all was well. Student groups trickled back to the classroom and said that they couldn't find the missions, or they couldn't log in with the code. I soon found out that I set up the second game wrong! I had to call everyone back, and we had to try again.

Although I was embarrassed at the time, I am glad it happened. It showed students that although I am a professor, I am human, and I make mistakes. I used it as a learning opportunity. When students came back to the classroom to reflect and share, I started the conversation by stating, "Don't be like me. Make sure that you set up the game properly for your students!" That seemed to put everyone at ease, and we were able to identify activities to use in our classroom using this tech tool.

On a more serious note, friends, I hesitate to even write this part, but I think it needs to be shared. In the summer of 2009, I had just completed my instructional technology online certification. I was so excited to have this certification and to really flex my muscles as an instructional technology coach at my school. I loved learning, and I still do! I wanted to keep growing and learning so I took a huge step: I applied for my PhD in special education.

I wrote my curriculum vitae (fancy word for a resume), crafted a cover letter, received reference letters, and found transcripts. I poured over the material to make sure I had it just right. I was a heck of a candidate. I had the paperwork, degrees, and certificates to prove it. I was passionate about working with students with special needs to grow, learn, and become independent. I truly loved what I did and to be honest, I rocked it. I worked with students using technology and integrated learning opportunities that were meaningful and fun. I worked hard with colleagues identifying and helping students with assistive technology and using it successfully in their classes and at home.

I sent in my application feeling all the feels (excited, nervous, anxious, happy, proud). I waited for what seemed like forever to receive a response. Then one day it came.

I remember that day, sitting in my kitchen and I was so nervous opening that letter. I was rejected. I didn't get in. I was in disbelief and shock. Surely, something had to be wrong. I even double checked the name – it was addressed to me, alright.

I started to doubt everything – I thought to myself, *I am not good enough, I couldn't get in, I couldn't hack it. It wasn't meant to be. I will never teach future teachers about the joys of working with students with special needs.* I felt embarrassed, dumb, and naive that I put myself out there, just to get rejected. In my head, the competitors for a spot in the PhD program were these super teachers who were incredible educators – passionate people who worked tirelessly to help students. At the time I didn't see this, but I was one of those super teachers.

I felt so sad, so defeated. It wasn't until I talked to my dad when I realized something interesting. Now, you have to understand my dad – sometimes he is pretty blunt. I called my parents in tears. I expected them to say things like, "Oh it's ok. Try again next year." Or "Why don't you apply to another school, honey?" But, they didn't.

Instead, my dad said, "Sammie this isn't new. You've been knocked down before. You got up. You got knocked down again, and you got back up. This is just another time when you got knocked down. Get up, rub some dirt on it, and dust yourself off."

He was right. This wasn't the first time I was knocked down. In the past year, I had faced other trials and came out stronger. They were preparing me for something like this. He was right. MY DAD WAS RIGHT! I never thought I would say this, let alone type it in a book. But, he was.

I started to reflect; what did I enjoy about special education? I liked seeing the students in the multiple disability class touch their picture on the SMART board and watch a clip of their favorite show. I really liked when they used environmental controls to make Thanksgiving dinner using a blender and a *Big Mack* switch. I liked helping with assistive technology evaluations and helping students find their voice. I liked working with the students in the learning support room, using a backchannel to ask and reply to questions during a *Bill Nye the Science Guy* video. I enjoyed watching students get brain breaks using Wii Video games.

I really liked it when we used the Wii for math class when students were learning about money. They would have to count out a certain amount for a cover charge before they could use the *Just Dance* game. Then they had to pay other amounts to sing and dance to other songs. As I was thinking about these experiences, they all have one thing in common – huzzah! Educational technology. I loved seeing how it made students excited, engaged, and independent with learning. In some cases, it made the impossible possible.

The rest was history. I applied to the Instructional Systems PhD program and got in. My research focused on how students with special needs can utilize augmented reality books for vocabulary word acquisition. It was remarkable – I had no idea that I was capable of this.

So, now what?

- Be ok with failing – it's going to happen. Come to grips with it now. Learn from your mistakes and move on. Don't dwell on them. Pick yourself up and keep going; it is just a speed bump along the way.
- Have a growth mindset. Sometimes this is easier said than done but persevere, as you will get through this. You got this, you've been through harder things than this and came out on the other side.
- Don't let one experience keep you down. Just because you have a lesson that fails doesn't mean you are going to fail the class, have to drop out of college, never become a teacher, and have to move back home with your parents. My friends, don't go down that rabbit hole. Instead, think of the big picture and reflect. Really think about what could have gone better? What did go well in the lesson? Focus on the positive, and reflect on the not so hot stuff of the lesson. You are learning, and it is a process. I promise you, you will get this.

🪄 Don't let one experience be your truth. For example, just because you taught a reading lesson in seventh grade and it didn't go very well, don't write off seventh grade as a grade you would never want to teach. Try it again. Give it another go. This is the same for a reading lesson that you taught in third grade, and it was stellar! The kids were participating, engaged, and you thought maybe you heard them chant your name as you left during a slow montage of clapping. Just because you had a lesson that was amazing in one class, don't stop there. Try another grade, another class, another school, another district. Keep getting experience and build your teaching repertoire. Build up your experiences and keep adding to it! As an amazing colleague, Dr. Connie Nichols, all around amazing trailblazer for education shares, "You should be so excited to work with kids that you would be the first one at the school if you

> could."

Always be kind

It is so important to show appreciation to those who have helped you along the way. For example, Abby Ross, a sophomore secondary English and communication education major, shares that "taking time to thank your co-ops or the teachers you observe is extremely important. I always try to include specific things in their classroom that stood out to me."

I try to do the same thing in my class with my students. I write a "thank you" note to each student during the semester. These notes are encouraging and usually pinpoint a specific act or characteristic that I observed as their professor. In fact, on multiple occasions students have approached me after they received their notes, letting me know that they needed that encouragement that day or it gave them a something to smile about during the week. It is so encouraging to hear that. Recently I caught up with a student, and she shared that she kept that thank you note that I wrote her above her desk – it gives her encouragement. Here is a Dr. Fecich fun fact: I keep all of the notes I receive from students, too!

You never know what is going on in someone's life or what is going on behind the curtain. I had one student share with me that during her college career she went through a traumatic experience, but she always found a safe and happy space in my classroom. She looked forward to class and enjoyed it. That was the most meaningful note of all. I still have it in my desk drawer.

Another way to show kindness in your classroom as a pre-service teacher is by doing the extra things. Mollie Carothers, a current edu-awesome middle school teacher in Pennsylvania, shares this story:

> I invested time after school and
> on the weekends to help the
> students with their clubs and
> fundraising. The relationships I
> built with students outside of
> school made developing lessons
> simple. By taking the time to
> learn about my students outside
> of school, I was able to go above
> and beyond in my lessons.

Relationships matter. Start by getting to know your students; go beyond just their names and likes/dislikes. Show up for them. Show up to their games, meets, or recitals. They will know you were in the audience. Be there for them. Even as a student teacher, you make a difference.

Another former student, Kaylee Strawhun helped her students show kindness. Here is her story:

> During my first student teaching
> experience, I have fond memories
> of making something I called
> "Mailbox Motivation."

It was a system in which students
could send affirmations to their
peers, and I could write
affirmations for my students as
well. It took extra time and
energy, but the results were worth
it. The "mailboxes" were simply
envelopes stapled to a poster
board, but the buy-in was huge! I
loved seeing (and reading)
positive words passed back and
forth between my students.

This is a great way to show kindness towards your students and cultivate it among them. What a great way to build classroom respect and rapport between the students and teacher!

If you were to come to the last day of classes in my classroom, you would be welcomed with music playing and games and activities around the room. I rearrange the room into several stations with activities at each station. Some stations have changed over the years, but here are some of my favorites:

- EDUC204-grams where students play *Bananagrams*, but all words must be related to class.

🪄 Charlotte Danielson Twister, where instead of saying "right foot, red," you say, "right foot, Domain 1." It is just a fun way to review the Four Domains of Teaching (Danielson, 2007).

🪄 Apples to Apples (GCC-style), where students play with cards created by my student assistant and me to reflect education major life at Grove City College. Some cards have professor names, specific assignments, technology tools, and other words related to our campus that only education majors get! It is a lot of fun to see how they relate the words together.

But the most popular station is the "Words of Encouragement" station. Around the room are sheets of paper, each with a student's name printed on it. Sticky notes and Sharpies are on the desks. Students take some time to write one another an encouraging word or two, a fond memory, something to lift spirits, or motivational quotes on the sticky notes and post it on the paper. By the end of class, each student has brightly colored notes on their paper. I then send each student their paper with notes attached via our campus mail. This is intentional for several reasons: 1) students love getting mail; 2) it arrives in their mailboxes during finals week for some extra motivation; 3) I can add a QR code on each paper that links to a video of class pictures set to music. This has been a wonderful way to end class on a positive note –

literally!

So, now what?

🖋 In the words of Michelle Tanner (Miller/Boyett Productions, 1995), "Duh!" Write a thank you note or two.

🖋 Integrate kindness into your classroom. Challenge yourself and students to choose kindness. You never know what it may lead to.

Always be intentional

Moments go by so quickly in college. You are there for four years, and although that may seem like a long time, it goes by so quickly. Make those moments count. Be intentional and purposeful. Remember this when you are walking down the aisles at the organization fair, being asked to sign up for every organization on campus. Think twice before you sign that paper.

Now, please don't think I am asking you to be a recluse in your dorm, only coming out for classes and meals and studying all day long. I am just letting you know that you don't have to say YES to all of the things. Don't overcommit yourself to all the great things going on around campus.

Don't be that student that signs up for the club just to have a list on your resume. Sign up for groups that you want to be a part of and to which you can contribute. When you are listing organizations and clubs on your resume, detail what you did, what you worked on, and how you contributed to the organization. Know now that you will have to say no to some opportunities that come your way, and that is OK. You need to choose wisely which opportunities are worth your time and commitment.

So, now what?

✎ Be selective about which organizations and clubs you sign up for. Really think about it. Don't overcommit yourself, especially during your first year. You don't want to miss out on an amazing opportunity because you have already signed up for three other things that day.

✎ Don't just sign up for an organization to fill up your resume. UGH! This is my biggest pet peeve. Don't do it. Resist that urge, my friends! Seriously don't be that person that joins a group and then does nothing in the organization, just to add it to your resume.

Always pitch in

For some of your education classes, you will be required to go into a classroom to observe. This is a great opportunity to work with students and learn. It is important to keep the mindset of "educate and engage" when you are conducting work in the field. These field hours are so important to your development as an educator. It bridges the gap between theory and practice. We can only teach you so much in a college class using case studies, but it is so important to see those ideas and concepts being played out with real students in real classrooms. Don't think of it as clocking time or checking off your hours during a 30-hour field experience. It is a 30-hour learning opportunity for you to grow! It is a time to interact and engage with children. It is a time to see what it is like to be a teacher, if only for a few hours a day. You get a sneak peek into the lives of being an educator, and that is a great gift.

Giboney-Wall (2018) shares that she tells her pre-service teachers that field experience is like an interview. This is so true; not only are you observing the teacher, but that teacher may be observing you and evaluating you. Use this opportunity to shine! Arrive on time and channel your inner scout: always be prepared.

The first time observing in the field can seem a little scary but, don't worry, you've got this. I want to share with you some stories from students who took the leap during an observation experience. Let's start with Kaitlin Gionta, who shares an observation she had during her first semester of freshman year.

> For my first field experience, my host teacher was very encouraging and excited to have me there.

He told me that they treated observations as student teaching experiences, so there wasn't any way I was just going to get away with sitting in the back of the classroom. Little did I know that I would be up in front of every class delivering some portion of the material to them and completely taking over two class periods to teach them.

Mind you, this was only my first semester of college – about two months into my studies – so I had barely begun Foundations of Teaching, yet I was confident in what I had learned so far to be able to stand and lead these students in their classes that day. That was the day that I knew for sure that I wanted to be a teacher.

Similarly, Emily Bach shares:

I would always ask the teacher if there were things I could do to help or to have practice teaching.

One memorable experience was a
five-day third-grade observation.
As I volunteered to help, the
teacher let me take over a class
project, teach Social Studies a few
days, and work one-on-one with
students who needed help. Even
though the assignment was to
observe, I couldn't help but jump
in and teach!

However, not every observation is this exciting.
Giulia Pucci shares this from her first field experience:

I was paired with an unfocused
student. He would talk out, walk
around the room, and not finish
his work. I scrambled for all of
the advice I had been given, but I
only had one semester of courses
under my belt, and the only
Education class I had taken was
Educational Psychology. More
than anything I kept thinking,
"Get to know your students," so I
ran with it.

I talked with him and paid
attention to the focus he could
hold.

He tapped his foot a lot, and I noticed his eyes gaze toward my mechanical pencil. First, I let him use my pencil. He was satisfied with that, but then he got distracted by his friends in the class. The students all have Kindles, so I grabbed his, and looked through the resources. I noticed that they had access to a media player, so I searched for some classical music and gave him headphones. Within minutes he was plowing through worksheets.

Giulia took what she knew and ran with it.

It is important to make the most of your time in field experiences or classroom observations. Every time I chat with a cooperating teacher for an observation or field, they are always impressed with the pre-service teachers who jump right in and get into it. They make the most of their time with students and get involved with their students' learning experiences. Yes, it is important to observe classroom management techniques, behavior strategies, and classroom climate, but if you can, I encourage you to jump in and get involved.

So, now what?

- 🪄 Get involved with the class and make the most of your time. Jump right into the class. Yes, there is a time to observe, but there is also a time to just get in there. Take the plunge!
- 🪄 Take the time to get to know the students you are working with. Whether you are working with them for a day, a week, or a whole semester, relationships go a long way.

G – Get Out!

"Venture outside your comfort zone. The rewards are worth it." – Rapunzel, Tangled

Get out (of the classroom)

Edcamps

I am sure that you remember the book *If you Give a Mouse a Cookie* (Numeroff, Bond, & Uzėlaitė, 1985). The story all stems from giving a mouse a cookie, then he wants some milk, and it goes on from there. The mouse gets into some trouble, and in the end, it all works out...it was all because you gave the mouse a cookie. This story comes to mind when I think of another former student, Katy Gibson. I met Katy as a sophomore in my Technology of Instruction class. She was jazzed about technology and excited to learn more about how to use it effectively in her classroom.

One afternoon in October, I was be-boppin' around Twitter, and I found a post about an edcamp in Pittsburgh. I had never heard of an edcamp (which is a free unconference, meaning sessions are planned that day), but it was close by and FREE. I sent out an email to a few students I thought might be interested in going and Katy was one of those students. In total, we had four students represent our college at Edcamp Pittsburgh in Fall 2015.

If you take a student to an edcamp, they will want

to start one themselves. So, the challenge was on! We had a small but mighty dream team to plan and execute our very first Edcamp, with Katy leading the charge. By the time April had rolled around, this team of pre-service educators contacted sponsors, received donations, planned the schedule of the day, created a website and social media presence, and hosted the entire event. The students took charge and really owned this event. Yes, by the end of the day we were all exhausted, but that was just the beginning of the legacy of EdcampGCC. This past April, we held our third edcamp, and it is all because of those few students who stepped outside of the classroom and took the time on a Saturday to learn and grow. Thank you, Hannah Sansom, Molly Carothers, Hannah Turk, and Katy Gibson for making EdcampGCC a reality.

Our edcamp has grown to include current educators, administrators, pre-service teachers, and higher ed faculty in attendance. We have also added several new experiences to our lineup of activities including an escape room, a tinker lounge, an alumni lounge, and an app smackdown. Giulia Pucci shares that during edcamps she can learn for the sake of learning.

> At edcamp, I get to set aside time
> for intrinsically motivated
> learning. I've found myself
> darting from session to session
> thinking, "Wow, I can't wait to
> use this in my future classroom!"
> or "This strategy is really going to
> impact my students someday."

Not only is the learning contagious at an edcamp, but so is the energy! When asked about her experience at edcamp, Jessie Pyle commented that one of her favorite things about edcamp is the contagious energy felt in the room by the attendees and lead learners. The energy at edcamps is electric, and it gets you pumped to get back into the classroom on Monday with new ideas ripe for implementation with your students. Each year we also try to give out grants to our attendees with leftover monetary donations. Edcamp has been a great way for our students to learn, serve, grow, and connect with professionals around them.

Edcamps are not the only way to get outside of the classroom and learn, but I am sure if you look around you, you can find workshops and conferences to attend! Attending a conference or workshop holds great value. You get to learn and connect with practicing educators in an exciting environment. By attending conferences, you get to hear about the latest ideas, trends, and techniques that real teachers are utilizing in their classes. It is also a space to network with educators where you can ask them questions, share ideas, and gain new perspectives.

Conferences

Catherine Root attended her first conference, MiniKeys in Pittsburgh, PA. By attending conferences, you not only learn about technology tools, but also how actual teachers are using various tech tools in the field. Catherine states, "attending the conference gave me many ideas about how I want to implement technology into my future classroom, and also gave me a built-in network and community where I can brainstorm, ask questions, and more with other educators." Don't forget to connect with those game changers after the workshop. You can even make one-on-one connections with administrators who can provide you with advice, interview tips, and the inside scoop on the job search.

Every year I try to attend PETE&C, a statewide educational technology conference in PA, and every year I like to take students with me to present or volunteer. At the conference, a recent graduate, Olivia Buirge explains, "you get a glimpse into what it is like to be a quality educator. There is so much that goes into teaching – it is not all about the content, but also about relationships."

In the past, I have had pre-service teachers present about topics such as augmented reality, Twitter as a PLN, ESL apps and tools, and more! Pre-service teachers prepare their presentations and deliver them to a room full of practicing teachers and administrators. That is a tough job even for a practicing teacher, yet these are pre-service teachers.

In my experience, not too many pre-service teachers attend conferences. Think about that for a minute. If you are a pre-service teacher attending or presenting at a conference, how does that make you different in this space? I have had students attend and present at these conferences, and be offered teaching opportunities – and these are juniors or even sophomores. That is powerful stuff!

Hannah Turk reflected upon her time when she presented as a pre-service teacher at PETE&C, stating that when she was a presenter, it showed her that she was currently a professional educator. Even though she did not have her own classroom, a degree, or letters behind her name, she was a professional sharing her knowledge. You are too! You are already a professional educator out there, with ideas to share with others. You are never "just" a student. You have a powerful voice with experience and stories to share. Never underestimate your voice, your ideas, your power. Go forth and share.

Giulia Pucci adds:

> Just because I don't hold a degree doesn't mean that my opinions and ideas are useless. At professional development events like Edcamp, I often find myself talking to teachers when they ask, "Where do you teach?" I tell them I'm a college student and they're shocked! I don't think my ideas are particularly earth-shattering, but they are still impactful even though I'm not yet fully certified.

RJ Dula attended his first PETE&C conference in February as a volunteer. He really made the most of his three days as a volunteer and connected with many educators in the area. He really owned his experience; whether it was volunteering at the registration desk or presenting about educational technology tools, he took advantage of this opportunity to grow and engage during this conference. RJ describes his experience:

I learned so much about myself
and about educational technology
while there. To see other
teachers, pre-service teachers, and
even retired teachers and hear
their stories was inspiring and
motivating for me. It's
experiences and moments like
these that push, change, and
shape you. It was at this
conference that I realized I am
really being called to work with
educational technology.

Hannah Sansom, a former student and current teacher in Pennsylvania, shares about attending conferences as a pre-service teacher: "Attending PD conferences and experiences as an undergrad set me apart from peers. I felt more prepared regarding networking and putting myself out there."

Let me share with you another story. This one is about Jordyn Pistilli, a secondary high school pre-service teacher. We co-presented a poster presentation at #tretc17 about virtual cooperating teachers (more to come later). TRETC is a local, Pittsburgh-area tech conference where leaders, teachers, and administrators come together and share about educational technology tools, strategies, and techniques. It is a great day of learning and leading.

This was the second time Jordyn and I presented together, and she rocked it! She introduced herself to professionals, talked about her learning experience, and shared so many resources. Jordyn prepared and presented herself beautifully as a professional educator. She was selected to be a TRETC pioneer during the conference, in addition to presenting a poster session. Her role involved "intentionally corresponding with conference attendees over social media, tweeting meaningful content throughout the day, and sharing her experiences."

She was to participate in the closing session at TRETC where a few participants were asked to give a five-minute reflection on what they learned that day. Her main takeaways included meeting her PLN in real life and learning from everyone in the room. Jordyn did so well that in fact, one superintendent pulled me aside and said as she pointed to her, "That is one to watch." I couldn't agree with her more! As a sophomore, Jordyn is presenting and sharing in a professional space with other educators and administrators.

You may be thinking to yourself, *that's cool – how do I get into this gig?* I encourage you to ask professors, your PLN, or teachers in your area about workshops or conferences that they recommend. Then take some time and check them out – search to find out who has presented, and if these opportunities are something that might help you grow. If so, then sign up to attend! If you have already attended conferences or workshops, see what the process is to present. Maybe partner up with a peer or a professor to present if you are nervous. It is never too early; get out there – you are a professional educator.

> Challenge:
> Get outside of the classroom and go learn something,
> whether that be at an edcamp, workshop, conference,
> webinar, etc. Go get your learn on!

Maybe you are thinking something like, *I don't have anything to share or present about; I don't have my own classroom.* In the words of Dwight Schrute (Reveille Productions, 2013), FALSE. Everyone has something to share and say. Educators are looking to you as a pre-service teacher to share your voice and what you are learning about.

Ask yourself: what are you passionate about when it comes to teaching and learning? Is there a cool tool or strategies you just can't teach without? Maybe there is a neat tech tool you tried during a field experience, and you want to share it with others. No matter what you share, be brave and put yourself out there. Even if you don't get accepted to present, you tried, and that is something! It will prepare you better for next time.

By attending and presenting at conferences, students get outside of their comfort zone and really flex those professional development muscles. Students realize that they, too are educators of excellence. Mollie Carothers shares this advice when attending conferences:

"Much of this growth came from the networking I was able to do at the conference. By having an opportunity to sit with experienced teachers and hear their conversations prior to and following the official lectures, I gained insight on how the theoretical ideas being proposed could look in real-life classrooms."

You may have the heart and the brains to do great things, but sometimes you may need a little courage, too. If you challenge yourself to go beyond expectations during your college career, you will leave with the knowledge that you can DO amazing things and BE a professional educator. That, my friend, is a great piece of education you are not going to get from any textbook. It is accomplished just by going outside of yourself, challenging yourself, and defying gravity! Take a leap and try.

So, now what?

- ✐ Ask about conferences or workshops you can attend locally, nationally, or globally.
- ✐ Contact a principal in your local district and see if you can present a topic during a professional development day.
- ✐ Attend an Edcamp in your area. If there isn't one channel your inner Katy Gibson and create one in your area.
- ✐ Channel your inner Sue Heck (Blackie and Blondie Productions, 2018) and write a conference proposal. Then write another – try, try, try!

Get out (of your comfort zone)

Get comfortable with the uncomfortable. What I

mean by that is to get outside of your comfort zone. It is called a comfort zone for a reason, it is our safe spot. College is meant to stretch you and grow you outside of your comfort zone.

Well, there is no time like now to get out of it. One way to do so is in your fieldwork and observations. A fantastic colleague of mine, Dr. Jarrett Chapman, has an assignment for his freshmen education majors to complete by the end of the semester. It is simple – students must observe a school that is different from the one that they attended.

So often we go into classes or schools where we have personal connections. Don't get me wrong – that isn't a bad thing, but you may want to stretch yourself a bit. Get into a class or a school that you have never visited or where you don't have any personal contacts.

For example, if you attended a public high school in the city and you want to teach secondary English, you may want to observe an English class in a private, rural school. If you are interested in teaching online one day, you may want to observe an online class in your specific grade and subject area of interest.

Think beyond public/private or charter vs. online; think about observing or doing fieldwork (if you have the opportunity to choose) in a school with a different socioeconomic status than the school you attended.

Remember Abbey Mae Method and her experience? She went out of her comfort zone and went to an inner-city school for an observation. The students tested her, as many do with unfamiliar teachers; instead of leaving feeling defeated, she left feeling excited and ready to learn more. You never know what going outside your comfort zone will bring.

Field trips for all!

Remember those days in elementary school when there was a field trip? I remember as a kid getting ready to go and my mom would pack a special lunch. I would have to bring some special gear like sunglasses, a hat, or a jacket. When I got to school, the anticipation was almost unbearable until I got on the bus to go to an amazing place.

The point is that no matter where you go whether it be the zoo, a museum, or the city dump (my sister actually had a field trip to a dump in her elementary career), a field trip provides students with learning experiences that they cannot access within the four walls of their classrooms. It gets them out into the learning wild! It sets them loose to stumble upon learning opportunities. This is why the idea of taking students out of the classroom should not stop in elementary or middle school. When I can, I love to take my students on field trips to innovative learning spaces in the area.

I challenge you to visit schools that are doing amazing things in your area. For example, each year I like to take a few students to visit the Montour Area School District. Yes, they have amazing things at Montour like a *Lego* lab, a Minecraft lab, and a state-of-the-art augmented reality lab, but really, we go because it is an innovative learning environment that embodies a growth mindset from kindergarten through graduation. When we visit Montour, my students get a private tour of the schools and see kids' learning in action. The visit gets pre-service teachers thinking about strategies that they can incorporate into their own instruction. The purpose of this idea is to get you to "think outside the bun" and grow as an educator. The more and diverse experiences you have, the better.

So, now what?

- Observe and conduct instructional practice in a variety of field experiences. Please don't just go to your mom's school every time. Get out and live a little. See what it is like teaching in a different district. I remember my favorite observation when I was an undergraduate at the *Children's Institute,* which is a place for students with disabilities. I learned so much during that day, and it opened up my mind to a private setting.
- Get more hours than the minimum required. You should want to knock the doors of the school down to get in and work with kids. Do so in whatever capacity you can. Be creative and open minded too – try volunteering at vacation bible school, tutoring, summer camps, day camps...you get the picture.

Get out (of your regularly scheduled programming)

I am not saying don't take your regular courses; what I __am__ saying is to try out an independent study. I have taught several independent study classes to students that are based around their interests. A few of the projects students completed as a result of their independent study with me include a conference proposal to a statewide conference, a website geared towards students with special needs to navigate the importance of digital citizenship, creating a resource for a geometry class with augmented reality, and teaching a lesson to elementary students with Ozobots. I even had my students attend a STEM event in the city to learn how K-12 students and teachers are getting it right in the field of STEM education. Yes, a lot of my examples are tech related, but an independent study can also include research projects going beyond an assignment or more in-depth on a particular topic. You may want to investigate independent studies at your college to hone your skills and grow.

If you are from the go big or go home camp, check out Rebecca Krupp's story. Rebecca is a current senior in Elementary Education and Special Education. Below, she shares her experience of writing a grant for the Education Department through a private foundation.

In the fall of 2017, the GCC Education Department was blessed with a large sum of money from a private foundation. This is a three-year-long grant that is designed to promote community outreach for individuals with disabilities in the area. The funds are awarded to students who pitch their proposal to a panel, and the winners implement their ideas with the help of faculty advisors and community supports. Rebecca shares her story below:

> The development of The GeniusCorps was something I could never have anticipated.
>
> The program began as one of those ideas that I would talk about with friends, always imagining that someone would do it, one day. I had no idea that I would be the one to bring this dream to reality. In the spring of my junior year, the Education Department at Grove City College partnered with a private foundation to offer pass-through grants to students, and the opportunity got me thinking.
>
> With enthusiastic support from professors, the Dean of the School of Science and Engineering, and administrators from the local school district, I submitted a grant proposal for a lab-based STEM program for middle school students of all abilities.

Right before the semester ended, I was awarded the grant. That day, the dream of accessible science came one step closer to reality.

Following a naming contest presented on Twitter and Facebook, The GeniusCorps was born.

When I returned to campus in the fall, I began to develop the program further. Conversations with the Dean led me to learn about the insurance and liability surrounding events in lab settings and provided me with a chance to talk with insurance companies about the logistics of the program. Other preparations included organizing volunteer teaching assistants (TA), checking appropriate clearances to work with children, modifying lab experiences, and purchasing materials.

The process of preparing for a lab begins with an idea.

I would find a lab that I thought
would be engaging and
interesting and works to be
modified to be accessible for all
the student participants.

Simultaneously, I worked closely
with professors in the different
disciplines of science to make
sure the labs are safe, performed
correctly, and cover important
topics.

TAs were provided with an
orientation and a crash course in
the lab procedures and the
science concepts involved. Once
the lab was finalized and the TAs
were given their orientation, the
lab was ready to roll.

The week before the first lab was
nerve-wracking. I would think to
myself, *would the lab be ready?*
Would the students enjoy it? Had all
the liability issues been addressed?

As the students arrived, I went out to greet them as they got off the bus and welcomed them. By the time the hour had passed, I was confident that this program was going to be a success. Months of planning and preparation had gone into the hour of exploration and learning, and I couldn't wait for the next lab.

Students who participated in the first year of The GeniusCorps had the chance to explore microbiology by building their own microscopes and comparing them to ones in the lab.

They also learned about the chemistry of fireworks, the importance of pill coatings and medicine in the human body, some of the basic principles of physics, concepts in electrical engineering (including switches and open and closed circuits), and how to code robots using Python code.

I hope that students in the years to come continue to have diverse experiences in the STEM fields, just like the students did in the first year. As the labs progressed, I challenged myself by working on labs that covered topics that I had never explored.

As I entered these unfamiliar subjects, I learned the importance of having professors as mentors. When the electrical engineering lab nearly caught on fire during the troubleshooting process, professors in that department helped me to test the different components and figure out a solution to the problem.

During labs, I learned about the hidden talents of my TAs when two of them stepped up to help run the physics side. The TAs were volunteer students in a variety of areas, from education to science. These labs would not have been possible without the help of these volunteers. It really does take a village sometimes!

The GeniusCorps successfully completed its first year, and I am so excited for the second year to begin in the fall. I already began to search for funding to expand the program, and recently successfully secured funding for the second year.

This program exists to celebrate the abilities of young scientists and encourage them to develop their passions. By providing accessible lab experiences that allow all students to explore and discover, The GeniusCorps aims to change mindsets. Students who believe they are capable and who also view others as such become advocates.

They are the ones who will create a better, more accessible community for all people. Science labs were chosen as the place to develop these advocates because science, in part, exists to improve the lives of people.

If the community of scientists lacks diversity, then the solutions they reach will lack diversity as well. Participating in science is not about speed, but rather about perseverance. It isn't about knowing all the right answers, but about discovering them.

Scientists are perseverant, attentive, and passionate. The feedback was instant and enthusiastic. Students went back to their school talking about what they had seen, and teachers and administration were impressed by the accessibility of the labs and the energy of the TAs and students.

I could have never guessed that my time as a pre-service teacher would include designing and running a STEM program for students. The GeniusCorps has grown to be something larger than I could have ever imagined, and I hope that it will continue to influence the perspective that students have on science, and on their own capabilities.

This program has morphed from a grant that Rebecca applied for to a full-time job this January! She knocked it out of the park with her drive, passion, and love for this area, so much so that Grove City College picked up the funding for the program that they want her to stay!

So, now what?

- Identify your interests as a teacher. What gets you excited about teaching? Is it classroom design? A technology tool? Do you want to explore being an administrator one day?
- Chat with a professor about your interests and see if s/he would be interested in partnering with you for an independent study.

J – Inconceivable!

Vizzini: INCONCEIVABLE!
Inigo Montoya: You keep using that word – I don't
think you know what it means.
– The Princess Bride

In *The Princess Bride,* Vizzini thought that it was impossible for Westley to defeat his giant and outfight his best swordsman. He couldn't believe that Westley could take so many risks and overcome challenges to save Princess Buttercup. For some of you, you may be channeling your inner Inigo Montoya ("You keep using that word. I do not think it means what you think it means.") as I say this next statement. Please just bear with me here: activities that we can do today with technology were once thought of as inconceivable. Technology can help us to reach students in a way that can ignite their passion, creativity, and love for learning. But remember – technology without a purpose is just a fad.

For some, using technology in the classroom can be risky. When Emily Bach was student teaching, she tried to implement technology in a way that would enhance a lesson for her students. She planned a lesson for her third graders where students were assigned a specific planet to research. Instead of taking them to the library to read through books and search through stacks, she planned for them to use *Epic. Epic* is like the Netflix

121

for children's books. Emily set up accounts for each of her students, and they read along or read a specific book about the planet that they were researching. This instruction was tailored to each student and met them at their own reading level. Emily was able to adapt instruction and meet the students' needs all in one lesson, while each student took ownership of his/her own learning.

Emily Wilson shares a lesson that she team-taught during a Social Studies unit about maps to second graders. She used several stations involving technology in the classroom: block-based coding, an unplugged activity from *Code.org* curriculum, and a Dash robot to maneuver around a map. Students used a giant floor map and directed Dash around the map. Students had to follow directions, understand coordinates on a map, collaborate, and communicate with one another. This lesson not only utilized technology, but also the 4Cs encouraging students to communicate, collaborate, create, and think critically.

Emily Wilson had another rewarding experience while she was student teaching. She shares this:

> Just like in coding, robots use all sorts of inputs and outputs to operate. The robots that I decided to use were the Ozobots.
>
> These run on drawn lines, and I was able to give each table of students one robot.

Ozobots read codes based on color, and they are designed to change their color with the color line that they are running on.

To get the students excited about inputs and outputs, I had them change the input (line color) to change the output (robot color). The students were thrilled to use robots, and I noticed that after this engaging activity, the students were more willing to raise their hands and answer my questions on input and output devices.

The robots not only engaged the students and reinforced the concept that we were learning, but also encouraged them to explore this topic with real-world application. And the next day in the hallway as students entered the building, they were telling their friends about the robots, which meant that they remembered at least part of my lesson. I count this as a success!

Abbey Mae Method taught a lesson about genetic disorders as a part of a unit during her student teaching experience in seventh grade. During her coursework, she learned about service learning, and she wanted to put the concept into practice during her lesson. To accomplish this goal, Abbey Mae used <u>PostPals</u>, a website that safely connects students from across the globe. Students could connect to write letters and send small gifts to one another. Her students wrote letters to children in the United Kingdom who were diagnosed with the genetic disorder cystic fibrosis.

Before assigning each of her science classes a "pal" from the website, she had them research and learn more about cystic fibrosis to understand what the children were going through. Students wrote to their pals encouraging notes that included inspirational quotes and memes to help lift their spirits. Abbey Mae shares that after the lesson was completed, some "students asked about where they could find an update on their pal. I pointed them back to the website, where updates are posted. I was so happy to know that they were still interested, even weeks after the project finished!"

Olivia Buirge shares this story of a lesson that she taught during her student teaching placement in eighth grade. The topic of instruction was biomes. Olivia could have had students read from the textbook and answer questions at the end of the chapter, but she wanted to add some *edumagic* to her lesson. She wanted to create an engaging and active learning experience for her students. To do that, she developed a lesson using virtual reality glasses and the Google Expeditions app to provide a real-life simulation of various biomes.

After checking the VR goggles out from our

curriculum library, she researched the Google Expedition App and identified several biomes found in the different expedition scenes that would cover information from the text and engage her students in the learning process. Olivia student-taught in a school where students could bring their own devices. She instructed them to download the app on their phones and showed them how to place their phones into the VR headset. Students were excited that a teacher would trust them to use their phones in class and enjoyed the privilege of doing so. Every student used their phone responsibly, which contributed to the success of this activity. This was a great way to show how to responsibly use technology in the classroom as well as show students that there is a myriad of resources on your phone for you to learn from and enjoy.

If you were a student in Olivia's class that day, you would have visited a tropical rainforest, an alpine, and arctic tundras. When students placed the goggles over their eyes, they were transported to different locations around the world. For example, they saw wildlife and the landscape of the Borneo rainforest in Southeast Asia, as well as the various climates and land elements in the tundra of Greenland. As students viewed the scenes through the goggles, Olivia acted as their "expedition guide" and explained what students were viewing (the app gives a great explanation for each scene). The next day in class, she reviewed the specific facts of the land biomes to provide both an engaging experience and concrete information. The students loved being able to see real scenes of these beautiful areas of Earth. It was a great resource to bring the world right into the classroom.

Drop the Mic

If you want a drop the mic moment in your classroom, take a look at Katy Gibson, a 2017 graduate in the field of middle-level math and science education. She was the 2017 Student Teacher of the Year for GCC, and she continues to impact the lives of children. She is currently teaching seventh-grade life science and math in Virginia, and shares her story from a field experience for an upper literacy course she took during her junior year. During this course, she was assigned to write a unit plan based on the novel *Number the Stars* (Lowry, 1989). Because this novel is based on actual historical events, she really wanted to make an impression on the students and make it come to life for them. Katy shares, "I feel students read about these events, but never actually get to speak to the people directly involved. Students are always asking why they have to learn about certain things in school, and I wanted to find a way for them to connect."

Katy's quest to bring this story to life began. She started her research small scale by first contacting the Holocaust Museum in Pittsburgh to see what they would be able to offer her students. Unfortunately, she didn't have any luck there. Now it would have been easy for Katy to give up right there and think to herself, "This is inconceivable – it is never going to happen." But instead, she thought a little bigger. This is where a light bulb went off about how much of an impact it would be for her students to speak with a Holocaust survivor. The plan was set, she contacted the Holocaust Museum in Washington DC, and soon her dreams to have a Holocaust survivor speak to her class were almost ready to go. However, their volunteers came in too late, and she wouldn't be teaching at that time.

Once again, Katy could have given up and just went through teaching her unit without this experience. She could have given up. But, no! She persevered. She thought about the book and remembered that there might be a museum in Denmark, where the story was based. In a final attempt, she was able to contact the Danish-Jewish Museum in Copenhagen, Denmark. Talk about going big or going home! This was it!

Through her connection, she was able to set up a Skype interview with a survivor for her students. Katy was able to Skype not only a survivor of the Holocaust into her class, but someone who had a similar story to the character in the book.

But that's not all! She was able to open the opportunity not just to her class, but to the entire grade level that was reading the book. In addition, Katy worked with our Department Chair, Connie Nichols, to simultaneously hold a special event at our college, and an entire middle school came to hear the survivor's story! Students listened and asked questions through an interpreter from the Danish-Jewish Museum.

During this same experience, Katy used her PLN to continue this eduawesome lesson. She organized a lesson where students contacted Lois Lowry, the author of *Number the Stars*. Students wrote reflections of their reactions to her novel. Lois even tweeted back to a few students, who responded with a thank you letter. What an incredible story of a teacher's perseverance and meaningful learning for students!

Katy continues to bring guest speakers into her classroom. For example, in March she had a scientist Skype into her class as students were learning about animal adaptations. The scientist shared her work with fire ants in North America and chatted about her experience as a first-generation college student in her family. What a great added learning bonus for her students, inspiring them to go beyond themselves.

Challenge:
Break out of the ordinary lesson.

Let me share with you a story about STEM Day at a local school district. Keep in mind, this event was not at all an assignment or associated with a grade for students who volunteered to attend. These students just saw an opportunity and jumped on it. Just because this event was planned by a school district doesn't mean you can't plan something like this for an after-school night or event with a local district at your college.

Let's get into it! This event came into focus during a snowy night in November at a Pennsylvania Association for Educational Communications and Technology (PAECT) meeting in North Western Pennsylvania over onion rings and great conversation. This is where I met Codey Whitton and Lorraine Schaffer, a dynamic duo looking to integrate STEM into their school. Then the idea hit us – I had pre-service teachers who needed practical experience in the classroom with students, and they wanted to have ways to show students and teachers how technology (specifically STEM) could be integrated into the curriculum. We combined our powers and came up with STEM day in April after all the standardized tests were completed.

Cody and Lorraine oversaw getting the space organized and the day planned. The day was organized so that all students in grades one through six would attend the STEM day event during their scheduled library time. Six stations were demonstrated simultaneously, and the students could attend three of them.

Students were placed into groups based on their choices and rotated every fifteen minutes to a different station where they engaged and learned about a STEM topic. My job was to oversee the presenters. I emailed our education majors to see who was interested in running a STEM station of their choice, where the elementary students and teachers could learn more about what STEM was and how to integrate it into their curriculum. Several students emailed back that they were interested in attending, and they planned their stations.

We identified six stations: Makey Makey, Quiver app, Sphero, Merge Cube, Canva, and virtual reality. During each station, the teachers discussed career connections that could be made if you use the specific tools. For example, at the Canva station, we talked about graphic designers. Throughout the day we heard comments such as, "This is so cool!" and, "Whoa! Look at this!" Students were engaged with their stations and enjoyed exploring the tools provided. That day, we had very few behavior issues, and the students were excited to learn and engage with the technology.

Jessie Pyle demonstrated Makey Makey to the students. She remarked observing the students' faces light up when they understood how the Makey Makey worked. In one of the groups, the students were really into it, and together they figured out how to make a human piano!

All of these lessons and ideas could not have been possible without the use of technology in a meaningful way. Technology seems to change every day. I can't wait to see what tools and techniques will be available to YOU when you are a teacher making the impossible, possible.

So, Now What?

🪄 Remember that ol' Nike slogan "Just do it?" Well, do just that! Try something out whether that be a strategy, tool, or technique just try.

C – Cooperating Teacher Gone Virtual

"We teachers are rather good at magic, you know."
–Professor McGonagall, Harry Potter and the
Deathly Hallows

Ok, so you may be asking yourself, "What exactly is a virtual co-op?" A virtual co-op is a current teacher who shares their passion for teaching and learning, who introduces a pre-service educator to Twitter, and who provides the pre-service educator with an authentic space for his/her projects. A virtual co-op is someone who volunteers to guide and mentor a pre-service teacher, virtually through email, social media, and online correspondences. Virtual co-ops come from all walks of life. I have had virtual co-ops from around the world including USA, Canada, Turkey, and even Niger, West Africa. Not all virtual co-ops are teachers; some are administrators, librarians, or technology coaches.

Cooperating (co-op) teachers are educators that we visit during our field experiences in the local schools and districts. Having a cooperating teacher is fantastic as they provide pre-service teachers with real hands-on experience with lessons, classroom management, and teaching strategies. However, these experiences are often limited by geographical location. It makes sense, right? We can only travel so far to get into a classroom to observe or conduct fieldwork, we only have so many hours in the day. But, what if we take away those geographical barriers? What if we opened the world to our field experiences? What if we reached out to innovative educators around the globe and worked with them to create engaging learning experiences for students? Please enter stage right: the virtual co-op.

> Challenge:
> Make every time you are in the classroom in front of kids is a learning experience.

Before I dig deeper into what a virtual co-op is, let me share a little bit of history behind the virtual co-op program. I teach students about educational technology embedded within the framework detailed by Charlotte Danielson. (Danielson, 2007). I tie technology very closely to pedagogy for students to understand and ensure that it is being used effectively and efficiently in the classroom. It is so important to do this– you don't want to just use technology for technology's sake, but have a purpose behind it. Yes, technology can be cool and shiny, but technology without a purpose for learning is just a fad. It will go away, and something new will take its place.

The course with virtual co-ops is for all majors and levels of students (freshmen through seniors). I try to make assignments applicable to a variety of grade levels, subject areas, and certification areas– which is not an easy task. I dedicate time to the courses that I teach to truly plan with intentionality and reason behind assignments for my students to complete.

However, my course wasn't always like that. One piece of feedback that I received during the first year was about the authenticity of the assignments. In the past, I would have students create materials using technology tools based on a state standard, and that was that. No sharing, no posting it online, no feedback other than from me, the professor. It was pathetic. Oh past Dr. Fecich – shame! But as we know, educators reflect and refine. I think Tom Miller, recent graduate in PreK-4 said it best in a tweet, "Teaching reflections save lives: yours, your students' motivation and success, and your pedagogy." By reflecting we refine our practice and make it best for our students.

To be totally honest, I was struggling with this issue for some time. I knew that this course could be something amazing for my students, and I wanted them to have a wonderful experience. During the summer I attended my first ISTE conference in Philadelphia, where I met the amazing Marialice Curran. If you don't know her, add her to your PLN – she is an amazing advocate for digital citizenship and developed an iMentor program. Marialice would pair her pre-service teachers with current teachers using Twitter, mentoring and coaching them through using the social media platform for the power of educational good. EUREKA! (*signal lightning flash above my head*) This is where the idea of virtual co-ops was born.

Virtual co-op program for the win!

This program provides pre-service teachers with

experience beyond the classroom through authentic learning experiences and assignments. Abbey Mae Method shares:

> This was one of the first times I was asked to create materials for a real curriculum. In this class, I was challenged to apply the resources we learned about to very specific content. This prepared me to more effectively use those technological resources when I was student teaching and couldn't just choose content that easily fit the digital platform. I learned how to be creative in how I incorporated technology because of the virtual co-op and her classroom.

Hannah Mercer shared the importance of authenticity for the assignments. Having assignments that were created for real students was motivating and exciting; it had a clear purpose. It required her to put in more effort and work hard.

Megan VanKirk shares,

> I loved feeling like I was helping another teacher in her classroom, and it helped me understand what specific things I could do to make her life easier.

It was definitely a time-consuming process. Designing tools to help teach concepts in the classroom takes time. However, knowing that the tools I was making for my co-op would make me more aware of different technological tools, and could be reusable in my own classroom definitely made the time I spent worth it, let alone the fact that the tools I made helped real students in a real classroom!"

STEM K-2 teacher in Pittsburgh and virtual co-op, Melissa Unger, explained:

I think a powerful part of this program is that students are leaving the semester with projects they have created that could be implemented in their own classrooms. Each activity has been tested in a real classroom, and students get feedback from classroom teachers.

> Having a collection of "working"
> technology artifacts is huge! This
> program gives pre-service
> teachers the chance to experiment
> and test their ideas with real
> students.

Not only is creating authentic work a win for the pre-service teacher, but so is the feedback provided by the virtual co-op about the project. Naomi Shrom-Kuk shared that during her virtual co-op Skype calls, Mr. Matt Rogers would give her feedback and describe how the lesson or activity went in the classroom. Often, the virtual cooperating teacher provides feedback about how the activity went or sends pictures to the pre-service teacher to see the activity in action.

Abbey Mae Method mentioned that one of the most important features of the program was the feedback provided by her co-op, who helped her to design her assignments with a real classroom in mind. "As an inexperienced educator, I didn't always have the 'teacher's eye' to see the weaknesses in my own work. What may look beautiful on my computer screen could be disastrous in a real classroom setting."

Jordyn Pistilli shares,

> While I appreciated the
> opportunity I had to practice
> creating tech tools, I know I most
> benefited from my co-op's advice
> and encouragement in pursuing
> my calling.

He served as a mentor to me,
sharing his classroom philosophy
and real-life examples of how he
manages his classroom. I really
appreciated my co-op sharing
feedback regarding the tools I'd
made for his class and letting me
know what his students thought.
If there was anything I could
improve on, he let me know that
as well.

The technology tools may change from semester to semester, but the best practices stick. Anna Emmons shares her experience working with Dr. Joe Harmon, who teaches eighth-grade civics and a twelfth-grade history elective on the Holocaust. She shares how she learned not just about technology tools that she could implement in her own field of study, but also about teaching and best practices. She learned how to write questions– really good questions that make students dive deeply into the content. She learned through her virtual co-op how to engage students in the content of history in new and exciting ways. But most importantly, Anna shares that she learned how to...

...view history through the lens of
teaching it.

It was the first time that I was
able to look at history and say to
myself, "Ok, this is great, but
how am I going to teach it to high
school kids?" And in doing this, I
realized that my passion wasn't
just for history, but also for
teaching it. Dr. Harmon and I
talked about this once – he said
that first and foremost, you're
teaching kids, and you should
care more about them than about
whatever subject you happen to
be teaching. That's something I'm
definitely going to be holding
onto.

The intersection of relationships, passion, content,
and teaching are very powerful.

Virtual co-op for the win-win

The virtual co-op program also helps the currently
practicing educator. Here, s/he is able to obtain practical
tools that s/he can use immediately with students. Also,
s/he has a chance to try out the latest tools and eliminate
the worry of where to start with new ones. Shane Mills, a
high school math teacher, calls this win, "the reciprocal
learning that goes on between the veteran and pre-service
teacher." I couldn't have said it better myself! Think of
Oprah saying this phrase, "Learning for everybody!" and
it is so true.

Matt Rogers, a fourth-grade teacher in Pennsylvania, shares that when he first began as a virtual co-op, he was going into his eighth year. As he puts it:

> I started some habits that I
> promised myself I would never
> do, such as repeating the same
> instruction year after year, while I
> had put forth a lot of effort
> previously. With the changes of
> 1:1, Web 2.0 tools, and other
> PBL-style ideas floating in my
> head, the collaborative experience
> helped dust off creative
> instructional practices.

The fact that this program is at its essence, virtual, is an advantage when it comes to using technology to connect across the world. According to Kristen Nan, a third-grade teacher near Pittsburgh, Pennsylvania and one heck of an inspirational educator, the process and workload of being a virtual co-op are rather minimal when compared with the rewards of working with a pre-service teacher. The simple step of meeting virtually using social media and video tools models the fact that there is always a way to conquer barriers in education – your location does not have to define you.

Being a virtual co-op doesn't have to end at assignments and work samples, as Melissa Krenzer, a fourth-grade educator in our neighboring district, shares. It is also good food for the teacher soul. One of the aspects of the program she valued most was to share her passion and fire for teaching, growth, and learning. She also enjoyed sharing the power of being a lifelong learner. Learning doesn't end after you walk across the stage at graduation and move your tassel to the left. Learning doesn't end with an advanced degree– not even a PhD! I continue to learn and grow with my students each year. Be a lead learner: be someone who is always willing to learn and grow because it is best for students of all ages.

Kevin McGuire, a librarian in Pittsburgh, states that he learned as much as his students. His pre-service teachers shared a lot of fresh and innovative ideas, and it was great to see education through their eyes. By working with the pre-service teachers, co-ops have been given the opportunity to try out new tools, apps, strategies, and techniques. This relationship is mutually beneficial.

As Caleb Ritenour, a third-grade teacher, states, "The pre-service teachers gained wisdom and insight on curriculum development, and the cooperating teachers learned new tools and techniques for enriching instruction."

Kaitlyn Scully, a first-grade teacher in Florida and first-time virtual co-op, shares:

> I look around my classroom and
> see many of the awesome
> creations that my first virtual
> students provided me with;
> library guidelines, infographics,
> and a morning routine poster
> jump out at me.

Those resources give my students
the autonomy and structure that
they need. In addition to the print
resources, the pre-service teachers
created and curated a variety of
tech-related resources, giving my
students the chance to interact
with edtech tools that I wasn't
even familiar with.

Virtual co-op program for the win-win-win

Not only do pre-service teachers and the virtual
co-ops benefit from the learning, but so do the students in
the classroom. B.J. Kurtz, a high school Spanish teacher,
and 2018 Pennsylvania Teacher of the Year finalist,
shares that her students benefited from the virtual co-op
relationship by having access to up-to-date activities and
having a fresh perspective on a topic that she was
covering in her class.

Kristen Nan also shares that working with her
student gave her a new perspective and a different way to
look at a topic. She shared this example:

I felt I had an amazing plan
prepared with engaging stations,
but my pre-service teacher sent us
Google Slides with QR Codes,
which simply hooked my
students in through a simple
curiosity builder of the unknown.

They fell in love with QR Codes
and started making their own!

Kristen continues:

Oh, how the unknown sparked an
excitement. They enjoyed
knowing that someone who has
never even met them was as
invested in them as much as I am.
It ignited a curiosity and gave
them questioning techniques that
led to, "How on Earth can we do
more of this, and what would that
take to put in place?" They loved
comparing my methods to that of
the pre-service teachers, finding
ways that both sides could work
to make it even better. The new
spin on ideas was a big hit!

Pay no attention to the man behind the curtain...

You may be thinking, "OK this sounds great. But,
how is this done?"

First, this program would not be possible without
the volunteer virtual co-ops. You may now be asking
yourself, where do you get the virtual co-ops? Well,
honestly? My PLN! I post about the program on Twitter,
Facebook, and Instagram and ask for volunteers. I also
reach out to alumni and former students. The alumni are
the secret sauce. They enjoy giving back to the college

through gifts and talents instead of a monetary donation. By providing practical experience, mentorship is such a meaningful way to give back to a college of education and help raise up and guide the next generation of educators.

Anywho, I do a lot of heavy lifting in the summer to recruit virtual co-ops for the following year. Each year I have about a 75% retention rate of returning co-ops (I don't have any hard data on that...just a guesstimate). Pairing a pre-service teacher and a virtual co-op is not an easy task. It is like pairing a fine wine and a delectable cheese (who is the wine and who is the cheese in this scenario? I am not sure – you figure it out).

In the past, I would pair students and co-ops based on subject area and grade level. But now, I have my pre-service teachers chime in on the process. During class, I block off time where students review co-op biographies. Students document on sticky notes why a particular co-op would be a good match to pair with them. Pre-service teachers document many different reasons why the co-op would be a good fit for them including living in their home state (or teaching in a state that they would like to live) or hoping to be paired with a subject matter expert in the field the pre-service teacher hopes to work, among other factors. My favorite one was because the co-op had the same name and spelling of the pre-service teacher's name.

When I get to work on pairing students with their co-ops, sometimes I look at qualities such as geographic location, subject area, or future area of study focus. Virtual co-ops are then revealed during the next class in an envelope fit for the Oscars, and students begin their professional journey with their cooperating teacher that day!

Some students have even visited their virtual co-ops over breaks for observation and fieldwork. How cool is that? Abby Ross was able to meet her co-op in person at an ECET2 Conference in Pittsburgh. She shared that, "it was amazing to learn from him as a virtual co-op, and then to continue to learn from him when I met him in person at the conference."

Another student, Kaitlin Gionta, describes her experience of observing her virtual co-op, Mr. Kevin McGuire, for a day in his classroom. Kaitlin shares, "For me, this experience with a virtual co-op was beyond what I was expecting because it goes so far beyond what you do in the classroom. Yes, they help you with your assignments, but while you're communicating with them about their needs, you're networking!"

One truly great story from a former student, Tom Miller, described what happened when he went beyond the screen with his virtual co-op, Caleb Ritenour. Tom writes:

> My virtual co-op is one of my teacher role-models. I made the decision to go beyond the screen and visit him in his third-grade classroom, and that was one of the best decisions of my senior year.

I hardly contributed anything to
his classroom routines or teaching
materials, but I walked away
from that experience with a
repertoire of ideas and a
newfound understanding of my
role as a male educator. A few
things that I could only hope to
replicate in my future classroom:
a wall of books, a student-
centered morning meeting,
integrated technology, student
responsibility, reading
workshops, multi-tiered and
themed behavior management
plans, and a laid-back rapport
with students.

Not all virtual co-op relationships have been rosy. Sometimes issues arose on the side of the students, like waiting until the night before to email their co-op for a topic, changing majors after the drop/add and "checking out" of class, or deciding that education isn't for them and dropping the class altogether. All of those situations leave the virtual co-op hanging because the in-service teacher is counting on the pre-service teacher for quality and timely work. Other times problems on the co-op side, the most common being that the in-service teacher does not get back to a student in time for an assigned topic, or s/he goes away from the keyboard (A.F.K.) In these cases, I have the student create the project on a topic of their choice tied to a state standard. It is not ideal, but it works.

The best piece of advice I can give is to communicate. Communicate often. At the beginning of the semester, I have pre-service teachers Skype or Google Hangout with their virtual co-op. It's just as an informal meeting to put a face to the name behind the screen, to show them that hey, a person is responding to my emails. This seems to help with some of that communication barrier. During these conversations, I have had virtual co-ops give students a tour of their school or classroom or even meet their own K-12 students!

Matt Rogers shares that during the weekly Google Hangout...

> ...the direct access allowed me to really get to know the pre-service teachers, provide real examples, and see the opportunity as more than just providing tasks to complete. We even had the chance to hang out during the school day, so the kiddos in my room had a chance to interview and thank each pre-service teacher. Needless to say, both parties enjoyed that!

I know it might sound a little weird that I want you to Skype a teacher you have never met. C'mon. Yeah, I'm serious. It is one step in making a professional connection with another educator. Naomi Schrom-Kuk, Matt's partnering pre-service teacher, shares that before the Skype call she was nervous, but after a few minutes of chatting her fears vanished. She found that he was excited to work with her. She shares that Matt…

> …was appreciative of the work that I did for his classroom, and I was honored to be a part of it. It was an influential part of my growth as a professional educator as it gave me an inside view of Mr. Rogers classroom. Mr. Rogers was also completely honest with me when he was exhausted or had a rough week, when a lesson went well or not-so-well, and what upcoming lessons he was looking forward to. The experience allowed me to apply what I was learning in the classroom, and to see it in action and be a part of it!

Megan Vankirk shares,

> One thing I am very grateful for with my virtual co-op was the ability to practice professionally communicating with another educator.

I was emailing my virtual co-op
at least two to three times per
week, talking about the tools I
created for her classroom and
clarifying specific things she
would like included. I feel that
this practice made me even more
comfortable once I started student
teaching because I knew what
kinds of questions to ask, and
ways that I could create helpful
tools in the classroom.

This program is a great opportunity for the virtual co-op and pre-service educators to connect, collaborate, and create an authentic, meaningful learning experience. Also, the virtual cooperating teacher benefits from the materials being created by pre-service educators to use in their classroom.

So, now what?

> ✒ If you are a pre-service teacher, I encourage you to reach out to your PLN or contact a teacher in the same field that you want to be certified in. Start to develop that professional relationship. Ask him/her questions about best practices, how he or she approaches a topic in their class, or other advice.

Put on Your Ruby Red Slippers

"You don't need to be helped any longer. You've always had the power to go back to Kansas."
–Glinda the Good Witch, Wizard of Oz

I have always been a huge fan of the *Wizard of Oz* (Baum, 1900). If you ever stop by my office, you can see for yourself. It is only fitting that I selected this quote to bring our journey together to a close. Remember as you are attending classes, writing papers, and creating innovative learning experiences for children, that you've always had the power to be an educator of excellence – you just had to learn it for yourself.

> Challenge:
> Let your inner *edumagic* shine through what you do and make the ordinary assignment extraordinary!

I encourage you to try something new in the classroom whether that be a tool, technique, or strategy. Maybe attend an edcamp or present at a conference. Who knows, maybe we will meet each other down the yellow brick road of life!

Remember sharing is caring – show how you are letting your inner *edumagic* shine by tweeting out with #edumagic or tweet me, maybe, @Sfecich – I love to connect with educators. Whatever you do, don't be afraid to be amazing and believe in yourself. Click your heels three times – you got this!

References

Baum, L. F. (1900). *The Wonderful Wizard of Oz.* Chicago, IL: George M. Hill Company.

Blackie and Blondie Productions, Warner Bros. (Producer). (2018). *The Middle [Television series].* Hollywood, CA: American Broadcasting Company.

Blumengarten, J. (n.d.). Education Chats. Retrieved June 23, 2018, from https://sites.google.com/site/twittereducationchats/education-chat-calendar

Breakout EDU. (2018). Retrieved 31 May 2018, from https://www.breakoutedu.com/

Burgess, D. (2012). *Teach like a Pirate: Increase Student Engagement, Boost Your Creativity, and Transform Your Life as an Educator.* San Diego, CA: Dave Burgess Consulting.

Chumbawamba. (1997). Tubthumping. On *Tubthumper.* [Audio file]. Retrieved from https://open.spotify.com/album/0x3uUHhj8bCoM5Uzi5FNIv

Couros, G. (2016). Positive, negative or neutral? Crucial conversations on digital citizenship [Blog].

Danielson, C. (2007). *Enhancing professional practice: A framework for teaching.* Alexandria, VA: Association for Supervision and Curriculum Development.

Disney, W., Luske, H. S., Geronimi, C., Jackson, W., Driscoll, B., Beaumont, K., ... Buena Vista Home Entertainment (Firm). (2007). Peter Pan.

Dweck, C. (2014). Teachers' Mindsets: "Every Student has something to teach me." Educational

Horizons, (2), 10-15.

Giboney-Wall, C. (2018) Mind your Ps (and Qs): A pre-service teacher's primer for job searching during your program. *Job search handbook for educators,* 52, 19.

Hollis, R. (2018). *Girl, wash your face: Stop believing the lies about who you are so you can become who you were meant to be.* Nashville, TN: Nelson Books, an imprint of Thomas Nelson.

How I Met Your Mother [Television series]. (2005). Los Angeles, California: CBS.

Hughes, J. (Director). (1986). *Ferris Bueller's Day Off* [Motion picture]. United States: Paramount Pictures.

International Society for Technology in Education. (2016). ISTE Standards for Students. Retrieved June 20, 2018, from https://www.iste.org/standards/for-students

International Society for Technology in Education. (2017). ISTE Standards for Educators. Retrieved June 20, 2018, from https://www.iste.org/standards/for-educators

Kappa Delta Pi. (2016). Portfolios in the job search: busy work or competitive edge? [Podcast] Available at: https://ww2.kdp.org/ssa/menu/downloads/product.aspx?ProductNumber=PC_PORTFOLIOS2 [Accessed 24 May 2018].

Lowry, L. (1989). *Number the stars.* Houghton Mifflin Harcourt.

Martin, T. (2017, August 31) #BookSnaps Snapchat for Annotation ISTE 2017 – R.E.A.L. Talk w/Tara

M. Martin Episode 25. [Video file]. Retrieved from https://www.youtube.com/watch?v=_yfRNxNo 1Ss

Miller/Boyett Productions. (Producer). (1995). *Full House* [Television series]. Burbank, CA: Warner Bros. Television

Numeroff, L. J., Bond, F., & Uželaitė, V. (1985). *If You Give a Mouse a Cookie*. New York, NY: Harper & Row.

Participate. (n.d.). Retrieved June 23, 2018, from https://www.participate.com/chats

Reveille Productions. (Producer). (2013). *The Office* [Television series]. Los Angeles, CA: National Broadcasting Company (NBC)

Sackstein, S. (2016). Homework, friend or foe? [Blog] *Work in Progress*. Available at: http://blogs.edweek.org/teachers/work_in_prog ress/2016/05/homework_friend_or_foe.html?qs =%22busy+work%22 [Accessed 31 May 2018].

Snyder, J. (2018). Effective resumes for education majors. *Job search handbook for educators,* 52, 8.

Stanton, A., Unkrich, L., Brooks, A., DeGeneres, E., & Gould, A. (2013). *Finding Nemo.* [video recording]. Burbank, CA: Walt Disney Studios Home Entertainment, 2013.

The Princess Bride[Motion picture]. (2001). Santa Monica, CA: MGM Home Entertainment.

Toy story [Motion picture]. (1995). Burbank, CA: Walt Disney Productions.

Ward, R. (2017). An introduction to twitter education
    chats. [Blog] *Personal Learning Network*. Available
    at:
    https://www.edutopia.org/blog/introduction-
    twitter-education-chats-robert-ward [Accessed 31
    May 2018].

Whitby, T. (2013). How do I get a PLN? [Blog]
    Education Trends. Available at:
    https://www.edutopia.org/blog/how-do-i-get-a-
    pln-tom-whitby [Accessed 31 May 2018].

Special Thanks

Special thanks to the power players who contributed to this book.

Abbey Mae Method	Megan VanKirk
Abby Ross	Mollie Carothers
Amanda Ebbott	Naomi Shrom-Kuc
Anna Emmons	Olivia Buirge
Bri Phillips	Rebecca Krupp
Catherine Root	Richard (RJ) Dula
Derek Witmer	Thomas Miller
Emily Bach	Connie Nichols
Emily Wilson	Barbara Kurtz
Giulia Pucci	Caleb Ritenour
Hannah Mercer	Derek Long
Hannah Sansom	Josh Weaver
Hannah Turk	Kaitlyn Scully
Jessie Pyle	Kevin McGuire
Jordyn Pistilli	Kristen Nan
Kaitlin Gionta	Matt Rogers
Katy Gibson	Melissa Krenzer
Kaylee Strawhun	Melissa Unger
Kylee McLafferty	Michael Bertoni
	Shane Mills

...and a special shout out to my dad, Joe Horochak for all of his sayings!

About the Author

Dr. Samantha (Sam) Fecich is an Assistant Professor and Instructional Technologist at Grove City College in Grove City, PA. At Grove City College, she teaches courses related to educational technology and special education. In her Technology of Instruction course, pre-service teachers take a deep dive into the Danielson Framework for Teaching and infuse technology into each domain. Students work closely with a virtual cooperating teacher (a teacher from around the world in their major area) to create technology tools for use in their classroom – giving meaning to their work. By the end of the course, students leave with a digital portfolio and professional digital presence through Twitter. Dr. Sam's passion in life is teaching pre-service teachers and professionals about special education and educational technology. She takes great pride in leading our next cohort of special education teachers to learn, grow, and thrive in their future careers.

She received her PhD in Learning, Design, and Technology from Penn State University. Her dissertation work focused on using augmented reality to adapt a reading text for students with special needs using their iPads and Aurasma. Before attending Penn State full-time, she was a special education teacher for four years at Clairview School, which is part of the Westmoreland County Intermediate Unit. She taught two years as a multiple disabilities teacher and two years as a technology integration teacher for students ages 5-21 with various disabilities. Her work at Clairview School afforded her opportunities to work with many types of learners. As the technology teacher, she integrated technology into reading, math, science, and transition classes. She trained and worked with teachers regarding technology usage in their lesson plans to enhance student learning. While working, she obtained her educational technology certificate from Penn State University World Campus and an Assistive Technology Certificate of Learning from California State University.

On a more personal note, Dr. Sam Fecich enjoys spending her time with family and friends at the lake. Her husband, Josh, is a great water skier and her daughter, Summer, enjoys being on the boat and swimming. Sam also makes a mean chocolate truffle.

You can learn more about Sam by visiting her website www.sfecich.com. She also enjoys learning from her PLN so give her follow on Twitter or Instagram @SFecich.

Other EduMatch Books

Adversity itself is not what defines us. It is how we react to that adversity and the choices we make that creates who we are and how we will persevere. *The Fire Within: Lessons from defeat that have ignited a passion* for learning is a compilation of stories from amazing educators who have faced personal adversity head on and have become stronger people for it.

Follow *The Teacher's Journey* with Brian as he weaves together the stories of seven incredible educators. Each step encourages educators at any level to reflect, grow, and connect. *The Teacher's Journey* will ignite your mind and heart through its practical ideas and vulnerable storytelling.

Why do you? Why would you? Why should you? Through the pages in this book, Dene Gainey helps you gain the confidence to be you, and understand the very power in what being you can produce. From philosophy to personal experiences, from existential considerations to the very nature of the human experience, consider who might be waiting on you to be you.

CPSIA information can be obtained
at www.ICGtesting.com
Printed in the USA
BVHW041706120121
597662BV00006B/115